# Angling in Earnest
A Coarse Fisher's Guide

# Angling in Earnest

A Coarse Fisher's Guide

Fred J. Taylor

## Stanley Paul
London Sydney Melbourne Auckland Johannesburg

Stanley Paul & Co. Ltd.

An imprint of the Hutchinson Publishing Group

3 Fitzroy Square, London W1P 6JD

Hutchinson Group (Australia) Pty Ltd
30–32 Cremorne Street, Richmond South, Victoria 3121
PO Box 151, Broadway, New South Wales 2007

Hutchinson Group (NZ) Ltd
32–34 View Road, PO Box 40–086, Glenfield, Auckland 10

Hutchinson Group (SA) (Pty) Ltd
PO Box 337, Bergvlei 2012, South Africa

First published by MacGibbon & Kee 1958
Second edition 1967
This third edition, wholly revised, 1980

Set in Times

Printed and bound in Great Britain by
McCorquodale (Newton) Ltd, Newton-le-Willows, Lancashire

British Library Cataloguing in Publication Data

Taylor, Frederick James
    Angling in earnest.—New ed.
    1. Fishing
    1. Title
    799.1'2     SH439

ISBN 0 09 141420 2

# Contents

To Carrie with love

# Preface

When I first wrote *Angling in Earnest* in 1958 I was dedicated to the pursuit of bigger-than-average fish and I had no patience with those anglers who only dabbled. I was still of the same opinion when I updated it for the second edition in 1967, and I still believe today that *Angling in Earnest* was the correct title for a work of this kind. I still expect to get out of fishing about as much as I put into it and while I am no longer prepared to suffer the physical torture I once did in the pursuit of fish, I still take my fishing seriously but I am now a more tolerant person. I have decided that it is possible to be a *serious thinking* angler and to achieve results through a thoughtful approach. I put in fewer hours of hard fishing these days, but because I understand better the times when my chances are greater, I probably still catch as many fish per hour of fishing as I did in those early days of dedication. And now I possibly have more fun doing so. I never was a miserable angler; my devotion to the sport at no time prevented me from enjoying a hearty laugh in the company of good friends, but today, perhaps, my overall approach is more light-hearted. I have almost re-written *Angling in Earnest* and I at one time toyed with the idea of changing the title to *Fishing for Fun*. But perhaps that will come later.

Meanwhile I have to accept that *some* luck, both good and bad, is experienced by everyone who casts a bait. I have had my share of both, but more importantly I have been lucky in having good friends. They along with my wife, who has been incredibly tolerant of my whims and fancies, have made my angling life all the more pleasant.

I would like to thank the editors of *Angler's Mail, Angling Times, Angling Magazine,* the *London Evening Standard* and the *Shooting Times* for their confidence in me and for allowing me to use certain material and photographs in this edition.

I thank Maurice Ingham, Ted Andrews and Peter Drennan for

helping with the diagrams and Kevin Clifford and Al Pond for helping with the photographs. I thank my brother Ken for putting up with my moods for more years than I care to remember. And lastly I thank Dick Walker for a life-time's friendship and for talking me into writing my first words on angling. It was he who started it all back there in the 1950s and who changed my life from that moment onwards.

FRED J. TAYLOR

# Foreword
# by Richard Walker

When *Angling in Earnest* was first published it was apparent to all who read it that its author was not only a highly knowledgeable and successful angler, but also one who thoroughly enjoyed his fishing and the companionship of the friends with whom he shared it.

Since then, many things in angling have changed. New materials have brought great improvements in tackle and in the angler's comfort; new methods of fishing, new baits and new devices have been evolved. Fred Taylor, not only a regular contributor to the angling press and to a national newspaper, but also a consultant to the tackle trade, has kept fully up-to-date with these innovations, and this new edition of *Angling in Earnest* has been comprehensively revised. But while there have been great changes in fishing, there has been no change in Fred, and this shows in the book as much as it ever did. For Fred, fishing is fun, and as with some other anglers of long experience, much of the fun lies in passing on his knowledge so that fellow-anglers can have more fun, too.

Of that, his writing is a part; no angler can fail to benefit from reading what follows.

RICHARD WALKER

# 1 Approach to Angling

There are, in my opinion, three approaches to angling, and to get the best out of the sport, one should try to have some experience of all three.

First there is the natural approach. A study of fish and their habits, of water lore and underwater life, of silent and stealthy movement, and the finding of the fish before trying to catch them.

Secondly there is the scientific approach. A study of water temperature, air temperature, wind direction, cloud formation, circulation and stratification. It includes the collecting of data regarding catches and conditions over long periods and the application of mathematics to angling.

Thirdly there is the technical approach. A practical knowledge of basic methods and techniques, the use of various baits and groundbaits and skill in handling tackle.

Each approach can be successful on its own, but a combination of three is often necessary. Consistency certainly depends on all three.

I was once told that I take my angling too seriously; that I work too hard for my fish. People told me that a few 4 pound tench do not warrant three weeks' work clearing and groundbaiting selected swims and that a 10 pound carp is a poor reward for forty-eight sleepless hours of hard fishing in wet or cold conditions. They told me that fishing is only a sport and as such should not be taken as seriously as if my life depended on it. To those people I say that it is possible to be serious and still to enjoy one's fishing, but I am the first now to admit that there is a limit.

I can be as happy fishing in an overgrown canal catching small roach and rudd as I can spending a weekend at a luxurious carp pool. I am just as happy throwing lobworms to chub as I am spinning a yellow-belly for salmon. I like to fish alone or with two or three friends, but I have no objection to fishing in with several hundred others. I shall never acquire the manipulative skill of the Northern or Midland match angler partly because I do not do enough of that particular type of fishing, but I think that every specimen hunter ought to fish in an occasional contest. Likewise I think that match anglers ought to go out on an occasional specimen hunt. I do not mean just an odd day 'free-lancing' as it is sometimes called, but a complete weekend or several days in quest of one particular fish – a period of serious specimen hunting can be even more exhausting than five hours' hard match fishing!

We are all inclined to favour our own particular brand of fishing, but we should make ourselves conversant with the other fellow's brand every so often. In this way we shall do a lot towards banishing the bad feeling which undoubtedly exists in many places between the matchman and the pleasure angler.

There are anglers (and I know some of them personally) who would not consider putting a rod together unless there was a cash prize involved. There are also anglers who view the matchman with scorn and call him a 'tiddler snatcher'. In both groups these people are in the minority, but their attitude does not improve the relationship between

A match angler's stall

matchman and pleasure angler. I say, quite sincerely, that the matchman who fishes for cash and has never caught a variety of specimen fish is missing a lot of pleasure. Likewise the specimen hunter who catches big fish regularly, but who has never fished a match, would have his eyes opened if he did. He would see angling skill and a companionship among anglers that he did not know existed before.

Match fishing has brought about many changes in float technique, and today's balsa and polystyrene float patterns are largely the result of the matchman's thinking.

Many of those floats have been used successfully by non-competitive anglers in the pursuit of big fish. Just as many have been used unsuccessfully, however, in situations where a much simpler tackle would have sufficed. Here the technical approach has taken over from the natural approach, and the situation, if given thought, might well have been resolved without the use of a float at all.

It should be remembered that the match angler is confined to ten yards of bank space, whether he approves or not. He must make the most of that space and extract as much from his 'peg' as is possible in the time available. His thinking *has* to be different from that of the angler who can choose his time and place. He not only has to start fish feeding (often after they have been scared by the approach of several coachloads of his colleagues) but he has to devise ways and means of attracting fish from his neighbours' swims and holding them in his own. He cannot stalk his fish or set siege upon them, and the prevailing weather conditions have little bearing upon his allotted 10 yards of water. He cannot exploit his knowledge to any great degree because he is in no position to move from where he sits. Unlike the angler who spends whole weekends at the waterside in search of big carp, bream or tench, he cannot move around to take advantage of the sun's first rays or put his bait in the deeps or shallows as the occasion demands.

The development of specialized floats has resulted in extremely difficult fish being caught more often, and there is a place in every angler's bag for a range to suit the many situations likely to be encountered in the course of a season, but float patterns and techniques should not be decided upon before thought has been given to location, timing and stealthy approach.

If you can see a fish and are sure it cannot see you, the chances are that it can be caught on a bait presented on a completely floatless and leadless tackle. Only in the event that floats or leads are regarded as being essential to presentation does it become necessary to go deeply into float pattern.

Used with thought and with due consideration to each situation, floats are as essential as leads, shots and hooks, but they have their limitations and the most delicate float tackle will not catch a fish that isn't there. A study of the feeding habits and general behaviour of fish is usually likely to prove more beneficial to the angler than an in-depth study of terminal tackles. That comes later and with growing experience. Observation meanwhile is the key.

# 2 Preoccupation

In the early 1950s Richard Walker and I exchanged some correspondence. We discussed mainly carp, tench and pike, but it soon became apparent that we had similar thoughts about the feeding habits of other species also. We were obviously experiencing the same problems with regard to fish that were feeding enthusiastically in our swims and often under our very rod tips, but which were completely disinterested in our baits. We were in no doubt that they were indulging in an abundance of natural food and that they had become unaware of any other kind. I described them as having developed a complex with regard to certain small items of food. Richard Walker described them as being preoccupied and as this seemed to sum up the situation we found ourselves using this term exclusively.

It is an interesting theory, and there can be few fish, if any at all, that have not given indication of complete preoccupation at some time or other.

Carp, tench and bream, the accepted stillwater bottom-feeders, tend to become preoccupied with larvae of different kinds, and there can be few experienced anglers who have not seen the sheets of bubbles sent to the surface by fish delving into the bottom mud. The bubbles are smaller and more pronounced where deep silt occurs. Carp, tench and, perhaps to a lesser extent, bream, tend to suck in mouthfuls of mud, sift out the food and 'filter' the remainder. It is this filtering that causes the sheets of bubbles to rise to the surface.

There are times during the season when concentrations of larvae are heavier than others, and it can be frustrating to see huge carp upending themselves in the shallow water completely oblivious to any kind of bait or groundbait. It is equally so to see the oily calm water of a tench swim 'boil' with minute bubbles as the fish forage in the mud below. Pieces of rotten weed, even twigs, often come to the surface as the turning-over process continues. At such times very few tench are caught on orthodox, bottom-fished baits. Bream behave in similar fashion, but I am of the opinion that they do not delve as deeply or turn over the bottom as enthusiastically as carp or tench. The bubbles they send up appear, usually, to be larger, but this may be due to the nature of the bottom of the waters where I have witnessed them. Certainly it would seem that bubbles are fewer and larger where the bottom is of hard gravel, and generally speaking the preoccupation does not appear to be so intense.

It is, of course, well known that trout become preoccupied with certain flies or insects although the term 'preoccupation' is seldom applied to the situation. Brown trout are possibly more choosy than the popular rainbow, but a nymphing rainbow can often be hard to catch unless a perfect imitation is produced and presented correctly. There are exceptions, however. Rainbows, not strictly predatory, are at least aggressive. A rainbow can be teased into striking at a fry fly or streamer pattern, particularly if it can be made to pass close to the fish's mouth or in its immediate vision 'window'. It may take time, but a rainbow will often, out of sheer annoyance, forgo the natural insects briefly in order to deal with what appears to be an intruder. When brown trout are rising to a mayfly, the precision of their movements, their timing and their complete preoccupation, has to be seen to be believed. An artificial mayfly, cast to perfection, will take a rising brown, but despite the fact that fly-fishing is reputed to be easy during the mayfly period, there are times when only an experienced fly-fisher can hope to succeed. 'Duffers' fortnight', as the mayfly period is often called, seldom lives up to its reputation.

When the fly hatch happens to comprise tiny midges or other similar insects, the preoccupation becomes more intense and the presenting of an imitation nigh impossible. The smaller the food item the deeper the preoccupation. On the Au Sable River in Michigan, USA, dedicated fly-fishers use tiny flies dressed on size 26 hooks and tied to leaders of less than 1 pound test in order to deal with this kind of situation. Their casting skills have to be seen to be believed; their eyesight is incredible.

Predatory fish like pike and perch, and perhaps to a lesser extent chub, often show a tendency to become preoccupied with shoals of minnows or fry. It is odd that on the days in question, the attacks do not take place until the shoals of lesser fish are concentrated. Then the water erupts, small fish shower like silver rain in all directions and one assumes that the predator retires briefly to swallow the several tiny fish it has scooped up en route and to await the formation of the shoal once more. It is extremely difficult, if not impossible, to catch pike or perch behaving in this fashion. The drifting of the shoals of fry causes the strikes to occur in many different spots and even a bait dropped with deadly accuracy into the 'eruption' is seldom taken. Usually it has arrived a second or so too late, and as it is a single item and not part of a shoal, it is ignored or overlooked. The largemouth bass of the big compounds in the U S A behave in similar fashion when the shad shoals are moving. It is said that the bass work in groups and 'herd' the shad shoals before attacking and, having witnessed it many times, I believe this to be true.

An interesting fact has come to light in recent years, however, and since we in the U K had overlooked the possibility of it happening here, I have applied the American anglers' technique to the pursuit of our own pike with a modest degree of success. It is only common sense and we ought to have recognized the possibility ourselves. When the bass rip into the shoals of shad, they leave behind them numbers of dead or dying bodies and immediately return to 'pick up the pieces'. These bodies invariably float and those with life still left in them twitch and flutter on the surface. The American angler drops a surface lure into the area and, with rod tip and reel manipulation, causes it to pop and gurgle. The size, pattern or colour appears to be relatively unimportant; the surface disturbance is what attracts the returning bass. Lures with odd names like 'Wounded spook' and 'Dying flutter' came into being for this situation alone and it so happens that, on occasions, the same lures and the same techniques will account for U K pike behaving in similar fashion. It is possible that perch may respond to the same technique, but I have had no personal experience and can only guess.

Another form of indirect preoccupation can occur when groundbait has been used extensively to attract non-predatory species. Over a period (and this could mean hours or days depending upon the size of the water) great shoals of small fish may gather in one area in order to exploit an unusual food source. I have mentioned groundbait but, of course, *any* natural food 'bonanza' will also provide a source of great attraction. At first only the small, non-predatory fish will gather but, eventually, because those small fish are in turn the food of the pike, large numbers of pike will join in the hunt. Small pike are followed by large pike until the whole area teems with fish.

Again this is a form of preoccupation and despite intense activity in the area, hookbaits are seldom taken. To a lesser degree the same thing often happens when a roach swim is fed on the little and often principle with light cloud bait. The cloud attracts hordes of minnows or small fry which 'home in' on every handful as it breaks up in the water. Soon every fresh handful is accompanied by a minor eruption on the surface as a pike ploughs its way through the build-up of small fish. It is worth mentioning here, perhaps, that in certain parts of the upper Thames, heavy groundbaiting for bream brings about similar occurrences. The difference, however, is that bream and not pike are responsible. There is no doubt whatsoever that the bream of certain weirpools attack the accumulations of tiny bleak as they gather around the tight balls of groundbait. These bream are predatory. Peter Stone has actually seen bleak eaten by them but, as with pike and perch, it is impossible to present a live bleak in a manner likely to be taken.

Among those teeming, silver hordes, the odds against a tethered bait being taken are astronomical. Dace and roach occasionally show the same tendencies as trout, though not necessarily with regard to hatching flies. Spent daddy longlegs on occasions fairly litter the surface of some of our slower rivers, and dace become virtually impossible to catch as they compete with each other for what must be very succulent morsels. It *is* possible to catch them by letting an impaled 'daddy' light gently on the surface, but so much time is needed to catch the live flies and present them without damage that the success rate is very low. Added to this is the fact that dace are experts at stealing the fly and leaving the hook bare.

Richard Walker ties an imitation daddy longlegs with trailing legs (which is apparently their position on the surface) with which he has successfully taken many rising, preoccupied dace.

I have no idea what approach to make when dace have their noses to the wall taking minute items of food from the green silkweed that grows on sunken piles and concrete reinforcements. I have never managed to wean them over on to a new food; even the deadly maggot is ignored.

Falling elderberries will cause dace, roach, chub and even grayling to become preoccupied. I have watched from a high vantage point while incredible shoals or accumulations of all four species lie in wait for the berries falling from an overhanging elder growing from between the stonework of an old bridge over a narrow stream. For most of the year it is only possible to spot a few fish here and there along a 2-mile-long stretch, but when the elderberries are ripe, the preoccupation begins. It is fascinating to strip off a handful of berries and allow them to trickle into the stream. The water boils with activity and yet, nine times out of ten a berry hookbait, lowered in at the same second, is ignored.

In May and early June, eels living in lakes containing carp become very preoccupied with carp spawn to the exclusion of all other food. Where it was possible to catch them on dead-fish baits the week before, it is now almost an impossibility. They can be seen in the shallows on the spawning beds and the damage they do must be enormous.

Barbel show a marked tendency to become preoccupied with small creatures which they take from the river bottom. Larvae of various kinds are particularly abundant on stretches of the Hampshire Avon and Stour. I have watched huge barbel sucking in mouthfuls of silty sand and blowing out what they did not wish to eat all in the close vicinity of my hookbaits and 'free offerings' of lobworms and cheese paste, etc. It is easy to understand why such huge fish are very difficult to catch when you consider that probably the greater part of their diet consists of small creatures like shrimps and various forms of larvae and crustaceans. Mr Charles Cassey's 16 pounder which he foulhooked on a salmon spinning bait was found to have a stomach full of Alder-fly larvae.

There you have examples of natural preoccupation in most of the fish the angler is likely to seek seriously.

However, apart from natural preoccupation, there is another type which, for want of better words, I can only call unnatural preoccupation. It is possible, in fact very often quite easy, to cause fish to become preoccupied with certain baits merely by introducing them into the water in sufficient quantities for long enough periods. Fish which are not feeding at all can be induced to feed in this manner and for the short period during which they are induced to feed they often become preoccupied with the steady stream of baits which is being introduced. This is only temporary, but a state of affairs often arises on hard-fished waters, when the continued introduction of one particular bait causes the fish to become thoroughly preoccupied with it. It is also a fact that the smaller the individual items of bait are, the more pronounced the preoccupation becomes. For instance – a steady stream of bread particles may cause chub to become temporarily preoccupied with bread, but they will still take a large piece on a hook. This is not so with maggots. If sufficient maggots are introduced into the swim, chub will not often take a bunch of these same maggots on a sensible-sized hook. They will take a single maggot on a No. 16 hook – but I do not consider a No. 16 hook ideal tackle for landing a large chub. There are many more instances of this and there is no need to delve too deeply into them. I think though that we should try to prevent what I call unnatural preoccupation as much as possible by studying the waters a little more and finding our fish where possible, in preference to making them find us.

When fish are naturally preoccupied with very small articles of food, I think the only hope that we have of catching them is to try and preoccupy them with something else. Where possible we should try to offer them the actual item of food which they are eating but, failing that, try to 'wean' them on to another small item of food by introducing it into the swim in a steady stream.

Brandlings can be used as cheap particle baits to wean tench, bream or perch over from their natural food

In recent years, and largely due to American influence, sweet corn, maize, beans, sultanas and many other kinds of particle baits have been used to attract, hold and catch carp, bream and tench. Obviously the fact that large areas of water can be littered with these convenient (though sometimes expensive) baits accounts for their deadliness, but there is also the question of smell. Many corn or cereal baits are allowed to ferment in the hot sun of the U S A and, while the smell is vile to human beings, it is undoubtedly attractive to carp and other fish.

Years ago I wrote that a long-term baiting policy with particle baits might very well account for the extremely difficult carp of waters like Redmire Pool, from which the record 44 pounder was caught in 1952. At that time our own visits were only of forty-eight hours' duration and occurred, perhaps, twice a season. Most times the water was covered with thick green scum and completely unfishable, so it was small wonder our catches were few. In 1966, however, I described the sweetcorn approach as carried out by our American cousins and this was taken up, and improved upon, by some of our dedicated carp men with the result that more carp were taken from this and other difficult waters. A case of unnatural preoccupation paying dividends. Today particle baits are used widely for big fish of many species and in some waters trout pellets, with their peculiar odour are being used to prebait carp, tench and bream swims in advance.

There is little difference in principle, of course, between modern particle baits and the maggots, hempseed, elderberries and stewed wheat used by our fathers and grandfathers. There is one advantage, however, in that sweetcorn, beans and raisins are large enough to be presented naturally on hooks and tackle capable of holding big carp, tench, bream or barbel. Causing this kind of preoccupation, or, if you like, conditioning of the fish in advance, is in my opinion acceptable. I see no other way of achieving the main object of fishing for big fish, which is to give yourself a better than even chance of putting what you hook on the bank.

Particle baits are discussed more deeply in the next chapter.

# 3 Baits

The average coarse fisherman, not being a specialist of any kind and not hoping to set the world on fire with big fish, records, or tremendous catches, takes to the water most weekends with a small supply of groundbait, a pint of maggots, maybe a few casters, and perhaps some standby hempseed. If he's a tench, bream or barbel man, he'll probably have some worms as well, assuming he's been able to buy or collect them in advance.

## Lobworms

Some anglers are what I call 'worm-orientated'. That is to say they are well aware that, whatever anyone else says to the contrary, lobworms are baits acceptable to *any* and *every* freshwater fish that swims, including salmon and sea trout. They wouldn't go fishing without them.

This does not suggest that they are in any way *superior* to maggots or other baits, of course, but it happens to be a fact that, in many situations, they are a better proposition. Their main advantage, apart from their attraction to fish of all kinds, lies in the fact that they can be presented on bigger hooks and on tackle considerably stronger than that used for maggot fishing. And when it comes to hooking and landing big fish that's important.

Lobworms are not always readily available. Most tacklists try to maintain supplies, but they are entirely dependent upon the collectors, who in turn are dependent upon the weather. If long, dry spells bake the ground hard there's little hope of a regular worm supply, which is all the more reason why we should look after those we happen to have. And if we collect our own from wet lawns after dark we should take care to make sure that each one we collect is serviceable.

One hears talk of 'pulling' worms at night. It's an old expression and many worms *are* actually *pulled* from the ground each season. It doesn't take too much experience, however, to realize that you must not pull too hard. Otherwise you'll end up with half a worm instead of a whole one! You learn, as you tread lightly across paths and lawns, that vibrations send the worms back into their holes with incredible rapidity, and you need to move very quickly to nail a worm that's lying half in and half out of its hole. When you grab it, you're inclined to grab it hard and hold it tightly for fear it may escape, but that is almost as bad as *pulling* too hard. Pinched worms are damaged worms and although some may recover in time, they can go bad and ruin the whole supply. That's why it always grieves me to see anglers who are so particular about the way they buy, prepare and take care of their maggots and casters, neglect lobworms to such an extent that even their chances of survival are doubtful!

If you've spent good money on lobworms, bought from a reputable tackle shop, you can be fairly sure that you've got good-quality worms, value for money, and that when they're handed over to you they're in good shape. The collector and the tacklist have gone to some trouble to see to that; but from then on it's all down to you. And if you take your hundred worms, cram them into a small bait tin, and then fish all day in the hot sun, you need not expect to have many fit for use next day! Worms do not take kindly to being overcrowded, they do not take kindly to being overheated and they do not take kindly to becoming dry.

They need room; they need a temperature of around 45°F (there is latitude either way, 55°F is the absolute top limit regarding safety and, of course, there should be no question of frosting); and they need a reasonable amount of moisture. Accepted worm-keeping lore suggests the use of fresh moss, and many of the old books insist that lobs should be well scoured for several days before use. Scouring lobs in moss will do little harm provided the right conditions are maintained, but all this business is quite unnecessary, and it doesn't improve the worms at all! Kept in moist garden dirt (in a large, cool, wooden box) and/or moist shredded newspaper, lobworms will last a whole season.

### Brandlings

Brandlings take second place on my list of wormbaits and, although they're seldom rated very highly by anglers generally, they do provide a good substitute for lobs because they're usually readily available in old compost heaps and are unaffected by weather changes.

It's a dirty business trying to extract a good supply by picking out individual brandlings, but there's an easier way.

In any compost heap there are areas where the worms lie fairly thick-on-the-ground, and once you've discovered a hot spot it's easy to get them to *sort themselves* out. Break up the compost into small pieces leaving the brandlings intact, set it out in several small piles on a piece of flat ground (or in a wheelbarrow) and leave them strictly alone for ten minutes or so. You'll find then that you can remove the top layer of compost and throw it away because the brandlings will have moved down a layer, seemingly to avoid the daylight. Continue the process at ten-minute intervals and you'll end up with a whole pile of 'neat' brandlings which you can store in clean peat or leaf mould. From this supply you can pick out the best for hookbaits and leave the remainder for use as free feed or groundbait. Brandlings do not suffer too much, if at all, from rises in temperature but I believe it's better to keep them in the shade, generally speaking.

One word of warning. If you're storing large numbers of brandlings, or if you're taking – say – a biscuit-tinful on a night fishing trip, make sure there's a lid on top of the container during the night. Brandlings are very adept at crawling up the sides of a tin or box and escaping under cover of darkness. They don't *always* attempt it, and I cannot put my finger on the actual reason, but it happens.

I recall one night's bream-fishing on the Thames when my brother Ken and I lost in the region of 500 because we had no lid on the main container. By morning we had precisely nil. Strangely, though, those in the small bait boxes did not escape despite the fact that the lids were off for most of the time. We really know very little about worms of any kind if the truth be told!

There are, of course, other useful worms around such as marsh, gilt tails and so forth, but apart from the odd places where marsh worms and brandlings intermingle, I've never found them in any real quantity. I stick to lobs and brandlings because my supplies are reasonably assured, and because I have confidence in them.

There are so many ways of using both lobs and brandlings that it would take a book to describe them all, but I feel that the method of presenting whole worms is important and that too many anglers tend to worry about making sure they'll stay on the hook. They thread them on, or pass the hook right through them several times, and generally ruin them before they start. They end up with a lifeless gob of worm flesh without so much as a flicker of life to appear attractive to fish. True, fish will take them in this state, but I'm quite sure that a healthy wriggling worm looks more mouthwatering to a fish than a threaded-on, half-dead one.

Ideas regarding *where* to insert the hook differ. Some say through the middle; some, barbel experts in particular, say through the head; and I know several good anglers who say through the tail. I won't come down heavily in favour of any method, except to say that wherever you stick the worm, make sure that it is only hooked once and then only lightly through the 'skin'.

I'm not worried about concealing hooks. I'm more concerned with penetration when I get a bite, and I'm quite sure that burying or concealing hooks completely doesn't help a bit in this respect.

## Maggots

It's probably fair to say that there's no substitute for the popular maggot. It's a convenient and versatile bait, and it undoubtedly catches fish. Its success probably stems from the fact that it is used in large numbers as free feed or groundbait to such an extent that fish become conditioned into accepting or even expecting supplies. It's an ideal particle bait; but there are others which will suit certain situations even better and which will, in the long run, prove to be better for big fish. I do not suggest for one moment that big fish can't be caught on maggots. You only have to read about Avon chub and barbel catches to know that's not true, but I am convinced that other particle baits would succeed equally well if they were used to the same extent. Particle baits, identicals, seed baits, saturation baits, call them what you like, the fact is there are many products that can be used in exactly the same way as maggots. Some need preparing in advance, some can be used at once, but, in most situations, as with maggots, these baits serve as both feed and hookbait.

## Particle baits

To bait a swim with heavy meal, breadcrumb, or proprietary groundbait in conjunction with a particle-type hookbait rather defeats the object. Particle baits succeed because fish are encouraged to *feed* on them. They serve to attract fish, too, of course, but cloud and other groundbaits will also do this without actually starting the feeding process into motion.

So, what are these particle baits? Briefly, any commodity made up of large numbers of identical portions can almost certainly be put to use as bait. Wheat, sweetcorn, rice, barley, tares, beans, raisins are but a few and the best known, perhaps, is hempseed. In many quarters it is considered superior to the maggot and it's an education to see a good hemper go to work.

I have seen the water boil with small fish every time a few seeds touched the water, and I've seen that situation develop to a stage where the angler could achieve the same result simply by waving his arm as if to toss in more. That is a fact, and many hundreds of London anglers would be able to tell of similar incidents. They'd be the first to agree too, I think, that it's not the best way to go about hemping. No one surely wants the fish boiling on top.

Hempseed needs to be cooked until the white 'kernel' appears and many anglers recommend a pinch of soda to induce an attractive black appearance. Small ready-cooked quantities are obtainable from most tacklists also.

There has always raged a controversy about hempseed and I expect it will go on raging long after I've quit, but to say, as has been said, that it's an unsporting bait, is quite illogical. A grain of hemp, a maggot, a worm or any other kind of bait cannot be unsporting. It can only become unsporting in the hands of someone using it in an unsporting fashion. And it's possible to use *all* baits and methods in an unsporting fashion. You cannot blame the bait; but you can sometimes blame the angler for using hempseed like it's going out of style and possibly ruining someone else's chances of catching fish on anything else. But does that not apply to all particle-type baits?

Maggots, used by hundreds of anglers, gallons at a time, quickly saturated the Royalty fishery and made it next to impossible to catch fish on anything else. That was the fault of the anglers, not of the bait.

But here's where you meet the real snag regarding particle baits of any kind. In order to get the fish going, to win them over on to your particular offering, you have to give them plenty to find and exploit. If you took hempseed to some parts of the Lee you'd need very little to get the fish going because they already know about hempseed, but if you took it to a water where it had never been used before, the chances are that you would have to use a bushel bag before any effect was noticeable. Not always, of course. There *are* exceptions. I know one water where hempseed has been tried on several occasions in concentrated efforts with no result whatsoever, but generally speaking if you use enough you'll get fish to accept.

Do you spoil your own chances and those of others by introducing particle baits in large quantities like this, however? Are you going to end up with the fish refusing to take anything else? Higher and higher concentrations of particle baits could become necessary to catch fish, and that, in my opinion, is not a satisfactory state of affairs. It needs a degree of moderation, and it's up to the angler to weigh up the situation and consider the likely effects before indulging in the prolonged or concentrated use of particle baits.

Having said all that, however, let's not forget that the object of the groundbait and hookbait is to catch fish and there are many situations that lend themselves freely to the use of particle baits.

Stewed wheat, for instance, was once considered to be the ideal harvest-time bait, though why that should have been so is anyone's guess. Wheat was supposed to have found its way into the rivers during the harvest and for some reason stewed wheat was accepted as the 'in' bait at that time. Why anyone ever bothered to stew it I don't know, because if wheat had found its way into the river naturally it most certainly would not have been stewed! I very much doubt if the wheat harvest ever affected the fish in the river anyway, and I've proved plenty of times that stewed wheat is as good a bait before and after that time as it is during it. In fact, stewed wheat is a super bait for catching roach and avoiding minnows, and here's a situation where you need *not* feed heavily. Minnows can manage to take maggots or casters but they cannot manage a boiled grain of wheat. You can be fairly sure that any put in the water will be either overlooked or taken by fish big enough to take them; and in a roach-dace-minnow water that means only the roach or dace.

Wheat is filling, however, and should be used fairly sparingly; just a few grains at frequent intervals. Sometimes it pays to use a great deal of light cloud bait at the same time so that the minnows are eventually 'choked off'. It's a little dodge that works on occasions, and all the better if there's a wheat hookbait to deter them as well.

Cooking wheat to perfection could almost be described as an art and as I don't profess to be artistic, my stewed wheat will never be as good as that cooked in our household when my father used to take me fishing as a boy. His wheat had to be perfect and mother knew all about perfection! I've caught lots of fish on rough wheat, badly cooked wheat, soaked wheat, sour wheat and even on puffed wheat, but I believe having good, specially-cooked wheat is as important as having top-quality maggots or casters. It may just give you the edge needed for difficult situations.

I won't try to make the business of cooking wheat sound difficult, but I do want to stress the point that it needs to be cooked *very, very* slowly; so slowly in fact that you can see no movement in the pan except the occasional plop of steam. Most of the water should be absorbed in cooking and just at the precise moment when the grains begin to split the pan should be removed from the heat. From then on the wheat will continue to soften without splitting further and will cool off into a congealed, glutinous mass that really looks, smells and feels good.

A less satisfactory, but nevertheless practical, method is to fill a vacuum flask up to two-thirds full with dry wheat, pour boiling water over it and leave it to swell overnight. It doesn't often come out perfect but it's always usable.

In recent years I have been convinced that strong-smelling baits (such as sour wheat) will provide an added attraction and draw the fish more quickly. I say this after about twelve years of interest and experiment in this field and my results, plus those of many other anglers both here and abroad, convince me; but on reflection I can go back to before the war and remember experiences which should have put me on the same track then – but didn't!

The local canal then boasted a grain elevator where barges were unloaded of their wheat cargoes and inevitably a percentage of this wheat found its way into the water. Stewed wheat was the recognized bait in that area and it was not uncommon to take good catches of bream, and roach, there. We were smart enough to recognize the association between the over-spill wheat and our stewed-wheat hookbaits, but it took me some time to realize that the wheat did not necessarily have to be cooked. All it needed was a good soaking. Even then, despite the fact that some of my soaked wheat began to develop a noticeable sour smell, I did not put two and two together.

It took a visit to the USA before I began to associate the ghastly smell of soaked corn (maize) with the fantastic carp taken over there. Out in the hot sun great barrels of maize were left to ferment and after a few days began to smell to high heaven. So much so that handling the stuff (and everyone who passed by the barrel would take a handful and toss it into the lake) necessitated a scrub up with carbolic soap or disinfectant. That smell hung around for hours after the barrel had been disturbed, but there's no doubt at all that the carp loved it and were attracted to it.

This was light yellow field corn, similar to what we now call sweetcorn or corn on the cob, but it remained fairly hard even after soaking. I could not get this particular kind of corn over here so I experimented with maize from the local corn chandler. It never softened – even after a whole year's soaking, but it developed exactly the same kind of smell and on my very first attempt at baiting with it over here a friend and I hooked eleven carp in one night – something unheard of before on that water. We didn't land them all unfortunately and over the next few seasons we lost a lot more and came to the conclusion that it was the hardness of the grain that prevented real hook penetration. I tried cooking the stuff but still the outer skin remained tough and losses continued. I experimented with butter beans too – soaked in the same fashion and also smelling pretty high. Results were fair though not consistent with the number of bites.

Canned sweetcorn provided the answer eventually and while it's true to say that this bait worked extremely well straight out of the tin, it worked even better if it had been steeped in the juice of the strong-smelling hard maize. It was better in that it attracted fish quickly. There was no need for prolonged pre-baiting; it was enough to take some of each and introduce it during the evening before settling in.

There is, to my way of thinking, something extra special about canned corn. It is the ideal particle bait for carp because it's just about immune from all other small fish. Tench take it, bream take it (I even caught a fair perch on it one dark night) but small rudd and roach can't manage it too well. Carp love it. And it seems to me, and to a good many other anglers who've tried it, that in many waters carp will find it before any other fish do so.

And that I think is a pretty important discovery. I'm not suggesting it works that way on all waters; but it undoubtedly does on a great many. It usually takes carp quite a time to settle down to a particular bait, but they home in on 'sweet 'n sour' corn very quickly. Carp fishing is a slow game and anything that will help make up the carp's mind and speed up the bites has to be something worth considering.

Since those early experiments great shoals of bream have been attracted to areas baited with dry wheat which, of course, eventually begins to soften and develop its own particular smell on the bottom. Friends and I have tried it in waters very far apart and the general result has been that bream have been attracted to the area even though wheat hookbaits have not necessarily proved successful. It is, however, encouraging to know that you're fishing where the fish are!

Mention of strong-smelling particle baits brings to mind the fairly recent successes achieved with sinking trout pellets. These, too, have a great attraction for tench, carp and bream. Most anglers have seen the way trout behave when pellets are introduced into stew ponds and while that's an entirely different and artificial situation, there's no doubt that continued baiting with trout pellets will draw and hold coarse fish. But the whole principle of particle baits is then to some extent defeated because it's impossible to put a trout pellet on a hook! There are plenty of times, of course, when it's enough to have attracted fish to your swim. Bread stodge, for example, will draw and hold fish while you proceed to catch them on worms, maggots or other hookbaits; so it's not *always* essential to use an identical particle hookbait in a particle-baited swim. But there are many times when it is.

The best way round this that I know is to mix up a brown bread and pellet paste. If you soak some brown breadcrumbs, stir in a handful of trout pellets, and leave it to swell overnight, you'll find you have a paste looking very much like plum duff. It needs moulding quite a lot to mix it all together, but it comes out almost the same colour (and smell) as a trout pellet.

This paste can be used in substantial chunks if the fish will accept it that way, or if they're totally preoccupied with picking up trout pellets, you'll have to scale down and mould a small, pellet-shaped piece around – say – a No. 12 hook. It works, I assure you. I've tried it and caught both tench and carp that way.

Trout pellets are, of course, expensive and possibly not easy to obtain, but I am told that certain aquarists' stores sell them under the general heading of fish food. One thing is certain; if you plan a week-long pre-baiting session and want a convenient bait to do it with, trout pellets offer that opportunity.

I have still not even scratched the surface of what particle baits are all about, and I've certainly not listed the large numbers of proven and successful ones.

I'll name a few more here for you to think about and, bearing in mind the expense involved with regard to some of them, leave you to decide for yourself.

Butter beans, baked beans, dry haricot beans, sultanas, raisins, currants, dried peas, tinned peas and several kinds of soaked grain have accounted for carp, bream and tench over the past few years. The greatest success, I feel sure, has been with carp and, in my own experience, canned sweetcorn has proved the best particle bait. I know that some of my fanatical carp-fishing friends have done extremely well with raisins and sultanas and that they might just disagree with me. On balance, however, and taking into consideration the difference in price, I'll stick to the corn.

One other useful particle bait should be recorded here. Boiled rice. It doesn't always work but, in streamy water where roach are shoaled later in the year, it can be an exceptionally good substitute for maggots. Boil it until it's tender, then run it under a cold tap to keep the grains separate and prevent further cooking.

## Bread

I can think of at least a dozen rivers, or stretches of rivers, where, despite heavy maggotting, the best roach almost invariably fall to bread in one shape or form.

A dear old friend of mine, whose ability I always admired, would seldom take more than a billiard-ball sized chunk of paste with him when he fished. 'What do I need more for?' he'd ask. 'I *know* where the fish are, and I know more or less when they'll come on feed – why should I waste time and food trying to get them some time else?' He was right, of course; he was seldom wrong, because he knew the river so well. And he knew it better when it was low and clear. 'People talk about flushes being necessary to improve the fishing,' he'd say, 'but I know where to find 'em when it's low. What do I need a flush for?' Again he had a point. He knew the places where, in low-water conditions, the fish were bound to accumulate; and he simply sat there with a big knob of bread paste until one of them took it!

Like many old timers he knew the value of a loaf of bread and even today, despite the big interest shown in other baits, I believe that, if pressed, I would choose a loaf of bread in preference to any other single bait. Bread crust has caught me more tench and carp than any other bait. Bread flake, the centre crumb of a new loaf, has proved deadly for bream and big roach. Bread paste, and balanced baits made up of crust and paste, have both taken fish of most species for me. The long strips of shiny crust taken from a new sliced loaf have caught chub from several rivers. Tiny crust cubes no larger than a match top have taken big tench in difficult conditions. Matchbox-sized crusts fished on the surface have dealt effectively with cruising carp. Hollowed out, a stale loaf shell will serve as a container for the soft paste made from its interior crumb. It keeps moist, cool and sweet and the shell itself will still serve as bait or groundbait later.

There are many other baits to be considered, and in particular the natural baits found in or around the waterside should not be overlooked. Mention will be made of their use in the chapters dealing with the different species. In the meantime a short list of natural baits known to have been successful over a great many years is as follows:

*Crayfish:* chub baits par excellence

*Freshwater mussels:* carp, chub, barbel, tench, bream, roach, rudd, perch, pike and eels have been caught on whole mussels or snippets

*Loach and bullheads:* excellent deadbaits for chub

*Wasp grubs:* some care is needed in extracting the cake, but the prime grubs are excellent as hookbaits while the mashed-up cake and advanced grubs serve as groundbait

*Black slugs:* picked up during the early morning from long grass. Good for chub and tench

*Frogs:* large or small, but *dead* please!

*Caddis grubs:* found in cattle drinks and shallows in early June. Taken from their twiggy 'homes' they make superb roach baits

*Flag worms:* taken from the stems of rushes (usually those that have gone yellow). Good for roach and dace on occasions

*Freshwater shrimps:* difficult to handle but excellent for big roach

*Brook lampreys:* deadly chub baits. Found in stony shallows

*Elderberries and blackberries:* good chub and roach baits in season

I could now start a completely new chapter and list all the other baits not already mentioned but, for the time being, a few of the more popular and recently exploited baits will suffice. Otherwise this chapter will never end.

Potatoes for carp, cherries for chub, tinned catfood, tinned spam, luncheon meat, sausage, cheese and cheese paste for barbel and chub. Fish and chicken livers, fish roes, prawns, shrimps, cockles, fish portions and raw meat for several species including tench, bream and carp.

# 4 Terminal Tackles

In different parts of the country fishing styles have been developed to suit the local conditions. Generally speaking these styles are the result of years of experience and are thoroughly reliable for use in the waters for which they were designed. When they are applied elsewhere, however, they fail miserably. For instance, to quote a couple of imaginary but possible extremes, the one-shot quill of the northern canal angler would be hopelessly inadequate for the fast rivers of the south. The heavy sliders used in some of the wide medium-paced rivers would be out of place in shallow lakes.

It would be impossible to describe every conceivable fishing tackle and its uses, but there are a number of basic terminal tackles which may be adapted for use in a variety of waters. Understanding their function may help considerably the angler who is somewhat puzzled by it all. Let us start with the float tackles.

## Floats

Coarse-fish anglers have always been float-conscious but, today, because of fishing pressures, they are more than ever so. They carry many different patterns which, because of their accepted fragility, are usually arranged in sequence in special foam-padded boxes. The average angler carries perhaps a dozen or more patterns, each in several different sizes, and, although manufacturers' wide ranges have, in some cases, encouraged anglers to become collectors, it is generally recognized that each float pattern has, in fact, been designed for a specific purpose. Additions to the range have evolved through necessity rather than a desire to produce more floats. Owning a large collection of floats can be a pleasure in its own right, but it is an indisputable fact that, without certain patterns, certain fishing situations cannot be fully exploited.

There are overlaps where one pattern can be made to serve several purposes, and it is possible at times to compromise but, generally speaking, the float *designed* to cope with a situation is the one that does it best. This fact is not always readily understood and it is fairly commonplace for less experienced anglers to be seen using floats wrongly and in the wrong situation. It is of little use tackling up with an expensive specialist float for any other reason than the one for which it was developed. The fact that one angler caught a netful of fish using a particular kind of float last week is no guarantee that it will produce similar results this week – even on the same river! The whole scene may have changed in the meantime, and conditions of weather, water level and temperature may indicate an entirely different float technique, but despite this there are many anglers who still prefer to base their choice of float on the result of last week's match! In doing so, of course, they handicap themselves, for it is not the specialist float that achieves the result but the knowledge of how and when to use it!

And in order to acquire that knowledge it is necessary to understand the basic mechanics of float-fishing and to be fully aware of the float's special duties.

These fall into three main categories, none of which could be considered more important than the other, and they can be sub-titled simply *presentation, manipulation,* and *indication*.

All three functions are aimed at catching fish and, naturally, compensate each other.

The float carries the shots that are so necessary for casting the bait to the required spot and taking it down to the required depth. Presentation with regard to both distance and depth may, therefore, be regarded as of prime importance.

In rivers and streams the float can make use of the current to carry the bait to the fish and, by steering, holding back, and generally controlling its path, the angler can manipulate the tackle into the exact spot. Once there the float serves to register bites when a fish takes the bait.

Those are the simple, basic functions of a float, but the most sensitive float in the world will not work if it is badly loaded or attached.

Too much or not enough shotting will render it ineffective on all three counts; and even the correct *amount* of shotting, badly spaced,

F. J. T. float-fishing

may have the same effect. It would be possible to quote many examples of what goes wrong in so many cases but, instead, let us look briefly at one simple shotting example. An exaggerated one, perhaps, but it will serve to give some idea of how bait presentation can be affected by the float's shotting pattern.

Leaving aside float design entirely and thinking only of the shots below the surface, consider the great differences in presentation, manipulation and registration that can be achieved by spreading the shots evenly, or by bunching the shots near the hook, or by bunching the shots near the float. Think about it. Think about how these tackles will behave in still water, in slow-moving water, and in fast-moving water. It doesn't take too much imagination to see that there will be vast differences and that although these arrangements can all be adapted to suit certain conditions perfectly, there are so many ways of using them wrongly. Nevertheless there's nothing very complicated about it; it's mostly simple common sense.

Balsa and expanded-polystyrene floats are famed for their lightness and buoyancy and it is fair to say that, apart from design, these are the all-important properties of good-quality floats. But it should be remembered too that lightness and buoyancy are totally incompatible with strength. All good floats are light and buoyant and therefore they must be fragile. There is no such thing as a top-quality strong float, and any attempt to strengthen delicate English-made balsa floats by extra coats of paint or varnish makes them heavy and renders them less buoyant.

Coarse fishers accept this fragility and most of them are aware of the many ways in which they can be harmed. They try to avoid dropping them on concrete, or letting them flap against the rod when walking with the tackle made up. They do not cram them into boxes with leads and other tackle, and they are aware of what extra-tight float caps can do on occasions. Minor points these, but even slightly damaged floats can become waterlogged and rendered ineffective in a short time.

A more important, and perhaps not so readily understood, fact about fishing with light modern floats has to do with line strength. There are optimum line strengths for each particular float pattern (though with some latitude either way) but it is of little use trying to use many of them with lines of over 6 pound breaking strain. In many cases 3 pound breaking strain or less is indicated, and the fairly common practice of trying to use these floats on lines of 10 pound breaking strain defeats the whole object of delicate float fishing. It cannot be done. If the techniques concerning the different float patterns are to be fully exploited and understood they must be practised with lines of suitable diameter.

The simplest float tackle possible comprises a tiny quill which is cocked by a single shot. It is used in still or nearly still waters – mostly canals – and is extremely sensitive. It is used with gossamer tackle and because of its extreme lightness it cannot be cast far. Generally speaking, this is an advantage, however, because bites on this tackle are usually registered very quickly. This means that the angler has to strike quickly and with only a short amount of line out he is able to do so.

This simple tackle can be modified in a number of ways by alterations to the size or shape of the float and also by altering the position of the shot. Usually the rig is adjusted so that the bait is just touching the bottom and the shot pinched on a few inches above it. Where bigger fish are expected, however, the shot and a foot of line may be allowed to lie on the bottom and one usually waits for a slower and bolder bite. When rudd or roach are feeding at near-surface or mid-water levels the shot may be slid up to within a few inches of the float. In extreme cases the shot may be removed altogether and the float made self-cocking by means of a piece of lead wire round the bottom end. In either case the bait (usually maggots) sinks very slowly under its own weight and appears to be unattached. If a small walnut-sized piece of moistened cloud bait or a few maggots, or both, are thrown in around the float the hookbait will appear to be but a part of a slowly sinking cloud of food. Bites will *not* be easy to recognize because they may take place at any depth and it is possible that the float may not move at all on occasions. You should be ready to strike at any movement of the float.

Further modifications may be made to this tackle by using heavier floats and more shots. This has to happen sometimes because longer casts are necessary to reach the fish. It is not desirable to pile on any more weight than is necessary; it is better to use a correctly shotted big float than to try to achieve distance with a small one. But it is essential that the shotting be correct. It's no use trying to use a big float which is riding high and half out of the water. No self respecting fish will pull it under! It should be shotted down so that only a fraction of an inch is out of the water and in this fashion it will respond to the most delicate of bites (*Figure 1*).

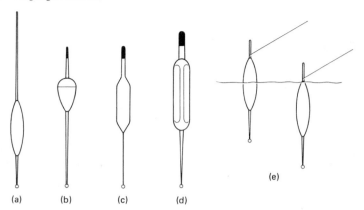

*Figure 1*

In windy conditions this float may be replaced by an antenna type. This has a cork, balsa or pith body placed *low* down on the stem. The stem is long and the float is shotted down until *all* the body is under water and only an inch or so of the antenna remains out of the water. This is a stable rig and is almost unaffected by wind. It will ride the waves and indicate bites very well indeed (*Figure 1a*).

While on the subject of still or nearly still waters, there is another entirely different rig which is used for shy-biting, bottom-feeding fish. Today it is referred to as a 'lift' tackle because the bite is registered by a lift of the float. Its extreme sensitivity is governed by the fact that the float does not have to be pulled under by a fish. It's a popular terminal tackle and one which can be absolutely deadly when used correctly. It is discussed fully in the tench chapter (pages 75–103).

All of the foregoing terminal tackles can be further adapted for use in waters of slow or moderate flow, with a greater or lesser degree of efficiency according to conditions. But it is doubtful if any of them will be of any use on fast and turbulent water. These waters require a biggish-bodied float which will not be sucked under by the pull of the current. The buoyancy must be nearer the top and they should not be shotted down too low. They have to ride steady in the current, and be visible from a long way off because they are generally used to carry the bait to fish well downstream of where the angler is seated. The extremely fast water of the grayling stream, for instance, demands a very buoyant and visible float. For this reason the simple grayling 'bob float' was designed many years ago. It is still unchanged and unbeatable today (*Figure 1b*). The wire stemmed float shown in *Figure 1c* is a useful alternative.

An addition to the accepted, big-bodied Avon float range, however, is the fluted float made of elder pith and balsa and designed, so far as I know, by the late Albert Smalley. These floats ride the water splendidly. They set up a resistance to the current which allows one to 'mend' the line without pulling them off course, but it is possible that their fluted shape sets up *less* resistance to a biting fish (*Figure 1d*).

These floats and other very buoyant floats are designed to carry a great deal of shot. This is necessary in order to get the bait down to the fish in the fast runs of rivers like the Avon. It is generally suggested that the float should be held back so that the bait travels in front the whole time. I have never believed this to be necessary and, as long as I am 'in touch' with my float, I don't believe it matters if the float happens to be pulling the bait along for a change. I am convinced that, at times, the bites are registered more quickly when this is so!

There is nothing to stop one of the old shot-dragger floats (still very popular in Germany incidentally) from being used to achieve this very end. Registration will depend a lot upon shotting depth and current, but in order to appreciate the subtle design difference built into the shot dragger it has to be understood that it is *meant* to present the bait at a speed slower than that of the natural current. I do not suggest that this *always* has to be the case. The decision to do so belongs to the

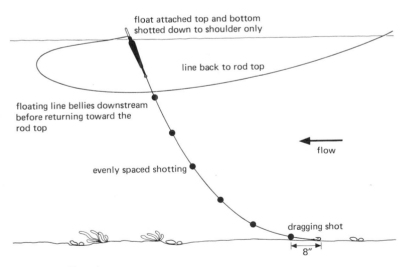

*Figure 2*  Shot-dragger

angler who has weighed up the situation. There are two ways of float-fishing a bait at a speed slower than that of the current. You can 'hold back' or you can 'drag shot', and the shot dragger with a little extra buoyancy built in where it counts allows this to happen (*Figure 2*).

The line can precede the float in a bow and literally tow the tackle down in a straight line. 'Mending' or sweeping the line back with the rod will tend to move a caught-up bait *downstream* because of the pull on the line.

The slider is used, in the main, for situations where the water is deeper than the length of the rod. Imagine a rod 12 feet long and a water 15 feet deep. With a fixed float it is virtually impossible to cast either accurately or very far. So a sliding float, which fishes at the correct depth once it has been cast, makes the job a lot easier. Because the float slides freely on the line its weight is added to that of the shots needed to cock it. This allows the tackle to be punched out because all the weight is bulked together towards the terminal point.

Some sliding floats have two free-running rings attached top and bottom; others slide on the bottom ring only. This means that almost any float could be converted into a slider at a push, but obviously those designed especially for the purpose will be best. In an emergency a simple ducker or antenna will suffice. The bottom ring attachment will allow them to slide freely on the line until contact is made with the nylon stop tied on the line at the correct depth setting.

This nylon stop will pass through the rod rings but will hold the float at the right depth because it cannot pass through the float ring (*Figure 3*).

Shotting patterns vary, of course, but because it is necessary to concentrate all the weight together to assist casting, most of the shots will have to be pinched on in the bottom quarter of the terminal length. It's all variable, however, and some adjustments will be required to suit different situations; but it should be obvious that shotting *up* the line will defeat the object of the slider.

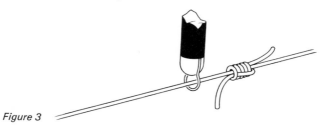

*Figure 3*

After casting, the float will slide up the line to the stop and this is then moved up or down to the correct depth setting.

In windy conditions put the rod tip under water briefly and sink the line to prevent it from being blown across the surface.

Traditional antenna floats have, for many years, been recommended for use in windy conditions on still waters, and many anglers still succeed in using them well for this particular situation. Bite registration on these wind-tossed creations are based purely and simply on a now-you-see-it-now-you-don't basis. The slender antenna rides the wave, disappears in the trough and reappears on the next wave. It is only when it *fails* to reappear that a bite is indicated, by which time it is often too late!

The plastic antenna float is designed not to cope with rough conditions but rather to produce better bites in calm or fairly calm conditions. There is nothing magic about plastic but in this case it *does* magnify bites because it is thinner than the traditional cane or quill

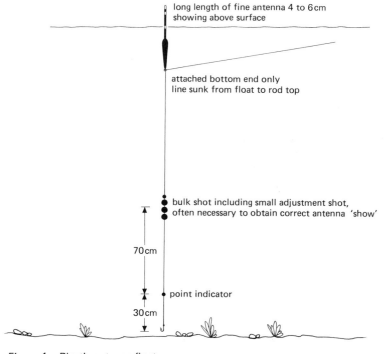

*Figure 4*    Plastic antenna float

used on other floats. The material itself is not important except that it can be used in very thin sections without loss of strength. Traditional materials shaved down to such fine limits would be too fragile to use effectively, and as the bite registration (or float movement) varies according to the thickness or otherwise of the float's antenna, it is essential to use the thinnest section possible (*Figure 4*).

The matchman's method of hitting fast or shy bites is to 'dot' them. This literally means shotting the float down until a mere dot remains on the surface. The nature of the bite, although still fast, then becomes 'softer' and easier to hit. Speed is still essential, but the matchman is well used to that and, as long as the bites remain within the scope of his own reflexes, he probably prefers it that way.

The ordinary angler who is not concerned with speed, however, and who may prefer to wait for longer periods between bites in the hopes of better quality fish, is not quite so keyed up and prefers to have more time. He may even need time to pick up the rod he has put temporarily into a rest. He may need time for 'finicky' bites to develop (as is often the case with tench and bream in high summer), and it may be of great help to him if he can see in which direction the fish is moving off with the bait.

Timing is important – not so much with regard to speed but more with regard to rhythm, and if bites can be slowed down it follows that good timing must follow automatically. This is the main function of a thin antenna-type float.

Imagine a fish pulling down a fat peacock quill antenna by about 5 mm and consider what effect the same bite would have if that 5 mm section could be *stretched* into a long thin section. The same *volume* of material would have to be pulled under but it would obviously take longer because it would have further to travel!

Fishing with 25, 50, or even 75 mm of fine diameter antenna showing out of the water actually induces long, slow, easy-to-hit bites. But, as always, there are limitations. The sacrifice in buoyancy at the tip of the float increases the tendency for it to drag under. In calm conditions the bait can be fished well on the bottom but, if a breeze springs up, dragging can occur, which will either sink the float or pick up weed or debris. Fishing just off the bottom helps but if this presentation doesn't suit the situation, a thicker, more buoyant antenna is indicated.

A fine, sensitive, antenna float needs accurate shotting, and very small shot sizes are almost invariably needed to achieve the correct cocking stance with the right amount of antenna riding clear of the surface. A big-bodied antenna might, for instance, take two AA, one BB and one No. 4 shot to cock it, but it may require a dust or micro shot to achieve the very delicate setting so necessary for this kind of fishing.

It takes time to set up properly, but the plastic antenna float takes away so much of the frustration of missed bites and makes many of them so much easier to strike, that this is time well spent.

I could go on writing about the many and varied floats on sale today but it would fill this book and another besides if I did. We could, perhaps, sum up the float-fishing situation by saying that there are two main basic types, top-buoyancy floats and bottom-buoyancy floats. Top buoyancy floats are *generally* used in rivers, bottom-buoyancy floats are *generally* used in still water. But there are overlaps. The ducker, for instance, is a bottom-buoyancy float that is used in rivers to combat a downstream wind. It is attached at the bottom end only and the line is sunk to allow the float to proceed downstream at the same speed as the current. There are also intermediate 'straight stems' (for want of a better description) where the buoyancy is evenly distributed. The simple peacock quill is a typical example. The important point to remember is that every float-fishing situation calls for some kind of compromise.

Small, sheltered ponds, for instance, seldom present any problems regarding float registration and even with fish on the finicky side, bites usually show up well on fine float tackle fished at close range.

It's a different proposition, however, when the water is vast and exposed and the tackle has to be fished at long range. Delicate bites call for delicate tackle otherwise they will not be seen in the chop; but long-range fishing calls for big, easily visible floats. It has to be some sort of a compromise eventually. Some of today's new balsa-or polystyrene-bodied floats with long 'antennas' and bottom buoyancy are ideal. They carry plenty of shot and register bites well at long range. I still see them being used incorrectly, however, i.e. attached top and bottom. There's *no way* you can fish properly with this kind of attachment. The float should be attached at the bottom end only and set so that about two inches of the foot-long antenna shows clear of the surface.

The float's length allows the line to be completely immersed under water and consequently out of the wind's drag immediately it cocks.

I find it better to slip the reel line through the bottom ring, slide it up

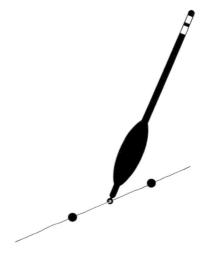

*Figure 5*   Trap-shotting

to the right depth setting, and fix it by pinching a shot on the line *each side* of the ring. These shots are better spaced at about an inch interval and if they're not pinched on too tightly, subsequent depth adjustment is simple. This attachment is referred to as 'trap-shotting' (*Figure 5*). The float, sliding freely on the line, is held (or trapped) between two split shots. It is an alternative bottom-end-only attachment that allows for a complete 'fold' of the float when a strike is made. The two shots help the float sit up quickly and sink the line below the surface out of the wind's pull. For practical purposes it is only really effective in depths up to 10 feet; after that it becomes difficult to use.

One or two points are worth watching:

For better casting it is advisable to place the bulk of the remaining shot in the bottom third of the terminal. That is to say, nearer the hook than the float. Lots of intermediate shotting can cause casting tangles.

Experiment is necessary regarding the final placings but a simple example would be as follows:

Depth 8 feet, two trap shots, one either side of float, bulk shot bunched 2 feet from the hook, final registration shot 6 inches from the hook. This is only a guide and placings will depend a lot on wind, depth, hook size and bait.

One important point. Do not use the trap-shotting method on floats where the bottom  ring is inserted into a soft balsa body. The shots will damage it beyond redemption during a day's fishing. Quill or hardwood bottom inserts will stand it; soft balsa won't. Despite the foregoing, however, I still like to make and use quill floats. Technically, of course, modern balsa and polystyrene floats are superior and consistent. If you lose one you can buy another that is identical and know full well that its shotting capacity is the same as the last one. But there's something nice about floats made of quill, and even today some of the more sophisticated floats on the market are made of peacock quill, which is remarkably consistent.

Swan quills are fun to own, fun to use, and fun to fashion into different floats. They can be used for many purposes, not the least of which is trotting a fairly strong and swirly current. You can be as technical or as artistic as you like regarding their preparation, but they *do* need shaving down with a razor blade or very sharp knife to remove the fibres, and they *do* need smoothing down afterwards with sandpaper.

It's of little use trying to rip off the feathers by pulling towards the fat end. You'll end up with a hole in the quill nine times out of ten.

Length and means of attachment to the line are a matter for personal choice. I simply use top and bottom rubber or latex bands, but if you want to attach a ring, or make provision for the line to pass through a permanent loop, it's easily done with a razor blade and a piece of whipping silk.

Big swan quills can be dyed and softened in boiling water so that they can be manipulated to shape. By picking two feathers and cutting off the hollow ends of each you can fit and glue one inside the other to make a thin, cigar-shaped, very buoyant float. You can glue in or whip on a bottom ring if you wish. Well varnished, this float will stand a lot of hard wear and tear. It is by no means technically superior to a modern float but it's nice to use and for many simple styles of fishing it is very satisfactory.

By leaving a fair length of the pithy portion attached, and attaching it at the fat end only, a good big swan quill will serve as an excellent float for fishing in the wind. The natural curve of the feather should not be straightened, but left to 'lean' with the wind. It's an old idea, but very effective.

Short, pithy portions of swan quills can, of course, be used as lift floats, and, if a little of the actual feather is left on it, the float will remain visible at long range in still water. It's then an effective float for rudd-fishing towards dark. Mention float settings and it is a fairly safe bet that the use of a plummet will be introduced. In many old books, the correct setting of the float by the plummet method was regarded as essential. Today there are situations where the technique cannot be applied.

If you're fishing a nice steady even-flowing stretch of river, a quiet hole or corner, or a still water of any kind, and you want to know the *exact* depth anywhere, it's easy to do with a plummet. If the float is set too deeply it will lie flat on the top; if it is not set deep enough, the weight of the plummet will pull it under.

That kind of plumbing goes by the board when you're trying to weigh up the contours and obstructions of a fast-flowing river swim. What you're really trying to find out is whether or not a float tackle will pass through unhindered – not what the *exact* depth is. There are many rivers where, apart from turbulence, little beds of streamer weed or soft patches of bottom milk weed render the knowledge of the *exact* depth more or less useless. There are ways of overcoming these obstructions and ways of presenting baits over them. It is also possible to anchor a lead on the bottom proper while the bait hovers nicely on or just over the weed. But these are fishing techniques which can be learned or put to use *without* using a plummet in advance.

The simplest way of 'plotting' the swim (as opposed to plumbing it) is to use a buoyant float, shot it up so that a fair bit of the shoulder remains out of the water, bunch the shot near the hook and 'sound' it all over its area. The picture doesn't form in a couple of minutes; it takes a fair time to figure it all. But by gradually increasing the depth and letting the tackle flow through absolutely unhindered and *not* 'holding back' (for the time being) you will eventually begin to figure the 'contours'. And you'll learn what those 'contours' are and how to deal with them.

There will be certain areas where the float can travel unhindered, so you can increase the depth until it catches up or is dragged under. It may be caught up on a single strand of weed, or a huge 'hillock' on the river bed. Or a big rock or a dozen other obstacles. What you have to do is figure exactly where they are and aim either to miss them by taking a different line of trot, or by manipulating the tackle over them.

Having learned as much about the contours as possible with the shot bunched, you will have a working idea of the exact depth in the important places. *Then* you can assemble your float tackle correctly and fish the swim with a mental picture of what the bottom looks like, where to hold back hard, where to feed and so forth. Expert matchmen may have different ideas, of course, but this idea has worked well enough for me.

### Freeline

I have, so far, failed to make mention of the situation requiring no float or leads whatsoever, and at the outset I should perhaps have suggested that every angler, before deciding which float to use, should ask himself whether he needs one at all. Floatless leadless tackles are usually referred to as freeline tackles and there are many situations where freelining is likely to be the deadliest method.

Let us look at a typical freeline approach. You are armed with a rod, a reel and a line of 6 pound breaking strain to which a No. 6 hook is tied direct. In a clear pocket among the bulrushes of a small stream are several chub. You can see them, but you have been careful to make sure that they cannot see you. Throw a big worm to land in their vicinity and watch what happens. The worm, completely unattached, sinks slowly under its own weight and, as it does so, the chub sense its presence. One of them (almost certainly the smallest) turns sharply in the water, there is a flash of its brassy side and the worm has disappeared. Now do the same thing with another worm, this time concealing the No. 6 hook attached to your line. It will land and sink slowly just like the unattached one offered previously and, if you have made no mistakes, it will disappear in the same manner – in a chub's mouth. The rest is up to you!

You do not *need* floats or leads for this kind of fishing; you would only spoil your own chances by using them. How do you think those chub would react if a gaudy float and a string of split shots landed in their midst? They would depart the scene, of course. And even if they did not, would they not become suspicious of a worm that sank like a ton of bricks as the shots dragged it down? That, basically, is freeline fishing.

It is practised by all kinds of anglers seeking all kinds of fish, and in many situations it is the deadliest of all. Even if the fish cannot be seen it may still be used effectively for bream, carp, tench, roach, rudd and other species. The deciding factor lies in the possibility or otherwise of presenting the bait *naturally* to the fish so, before you make up your mind what kind of float or other attachment to your line is needed, ask yourself this simple question. Can I manage without any at all? You'll be surprised at the number of times you can.

## Legers

There are times when float and freeline tackles are unable to cope with a particular situation and when the answer lies in the use of the leger. But how do you decide when to use a leger in preference to other methods?

The quick and simple answer is: when the water is too deep, too fast, or the range too far for regular float-fishing. Generally speaking those are reasons enough, though recent float developments have made it possible to use float tackle in many difficult situations and I think it's a good idea to look at it from a different angle.

The object of any exercise is to put the bait to the fish in an acceptable manner and obviously you could not use a floatless leadless tackle in the current of a fast and turbulent river. The bait would not get down, it would not stay put and it would be whisked away too quickly for the fish to find. Up to a point modern float tackle can be used to trot the bait through at the right depth and speed, but there are situations where so much lead and so much bulk is required that float tackle becomes unmanageable. The only answer then is to anchor the bait with an appropriate leger lead.

High winds also make float-fishing difficult in many situations in both still and moving water and, despite the superb floats available today, leger tackle is required if only for peace of mind. Very often, in these circumstances, better bite registration is shown on the leger and, with practice, it will be found that bites can often be *felt* better than they can be seen by using the touch leger technique.

Long-range fishing in still water calls for a streamlined leger rig and the Arlesey bomb used so effectively by Dick Walker in the 1950s is still the best distance lead available.

Extremely deep water is difficult to fish with float tackle; even sliders tend to be unreliable past a certain depth and a streamlined lead, cast out well past the desired spot and allowed to sink on a completely slack line will almost certainly make for a better presentation. The leger is being used more and more by match anglers today and what was once called 'splodging' is now referred to as 'on the lead' or 'on the bomb' by today's experts.

Many anglers still insist that they have no confidence in the leger simply because they use it only as a last resort when nothing is being caught. They catch nothing because the chances are there's nothing going to be caught anyway. If there are no bites forthcoming on float

Thames chub taken on a leger

tackle, in what is regarded as a swim suited to float fishing, it's unlikely that any fish will be caught on the leger. But because this happens, the leger is usually condemned by the keen float angler.

I feel that this is unfair treatment. A little more understanding of the uses of various leger tackles might have made all the difference to the catches of the anglers involved. Reams have been written on legering and the various forms of bite detection from swing tips to dough bobbins. Bite detection is a thing apart and what suits one angler will not necessarily suit another, but this is a minor detail compared with how the leger is going *to fish*. It is a detail, too, compared with the choice of swim and the species being sought. One would not, for instance, use an ounce lead, two yards out in a shallow, muddy-bottomed lake. Float tackle would almost certainly prove a better proposition – that or a completely leadless tackle. There is no point in using the leger in a swim which invariably fishes well with float tackle. Why handicap yourself? But, there are plenty of swims in both still and fast moving water where a leger and a *leger of a certain kind* is indicated. There are also plenty of swims where, not only is a certain kind of leger indicated, but a certain kind rigged up in a certain way! It will be impossible to list all the many rigs and their various modifications in one chapter, but I hope to show here that legering is not simply a question of attaching a sliding lead to the line, and waiting for a bite! Legering can be just as delicate as float-fishing and in many respects the arrangement of the terminal tackle can mean the difference between catching fish and not catching them. Let us look at a few basic leger terminal tackles.

Today, the Arlesey bomb is probably the most widely used leger in the business. It is used in various weights for practically all forms of legering, but its chief function is long-range legering in still waters. The swivelled, streamlined shape allows for long casting without tangling and for free passage of the line irrespective of the settling angle. The fact that its virtues were recognized and eventually applied to rivers and other waters was neither considered nor intended in the first place. But today it is our most versatile leger lead. How it is best put to use on fast waters and for various species of fish will take some telling for it can be put to a hundred uses.

Firstly, as a simple sliding leger, it is cast across and slightly downstream. It is allowed to roll slowly across the current until it finds its own settling place, where it is allowed to fish. After a time, if the rod is lifted slightly and a yard of slack line given, the leger will move (and with it the bait) into another position. At all times its efficiency is dependent on the current and for this reason it is essential that the correct sized lead be used. Too heavy, and the lead will 'splodge' in the middle of the river and there will be no feeling of being in touch with the bait. Too light, and the lead will swing across the current much too quickly and the bait will not 'fish' properly. To be right it should come across with a slow, bumping roll until it settles.

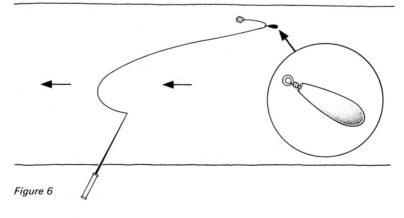

*Figure 6*

If it *is* right you may often expect bites *before* it settles! But do not believe with absolute certainty that the bite of a fish pulls the line *through* the ring of the swivel simply because it is intended that it should! Look at *Figure 6* and see how the line behaves in fast water.

You will see that it is not necessarily so. Hence the need again for the correct sized lead. It should be so delicately settled on the bottom that even the smallest fish will move it.

### Link legers

Unfortunately there are rather big variations in the sizes of Arlesey bombs. There is one weighing an ounce, there is one weighing $\frac{1}{8}$ ounce (a recent welcome addition to the range) but, generally speaking, the different sizes vary by quarter ounces. This means that the adjustment to the leger tackle is not fine enough if Arlesey bombs are used exclusively. Realizing this some years ago, I began to use links of nylon with a swivel attached and to these links I pinched a number of swan shots. These could be added to or removed one at a time until the correct balance was achieved. Sometimes even smaller shots were used and on certain occasions a twist of lead was added to achieve real accuracy.

This idea was extremely successful, and later Richard Walker suggested that there might not be any real need for the swivel. Since then we have dispensed with it almost completely and nowadays we simply fold the nylon link over the reel line and attach the appropriate number of shots. It is, to my way of thinking, the most useful of all leger rigs and there are very few occasions and few water conditions when it cannot be used successfully (*Figure 7*).

*Figure 8* shows an alternative attachment using a float cap for a quick changeover to float tackle if necessary.

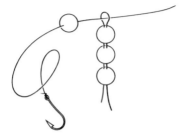

Figure 7

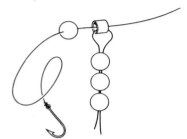

Figure 8

## Other leger weights

There *are* times, however, when it is necessary to have the leger stay put where it is cast. It is not always possible to 'roll' a leger into place and an accurate cast to the exact spot is essential. Once there, the lead and bait must settle quickly and be heavy enough to defeat the current which is continually trying to wash it away.

There are many circumstances where this sort of situation may be encountered. Perhaps the best instance I can give is of a chub hole underneath a bush on the opposite bank of the river. The midstream current will whisk away all but the heaviest of leads and it is necessary to use one which holds bottom well. Therefore it needs to be flat rather than round. There are specially designed pyramid-shaped leads for this purpose. They do the job extremely well.

One of the older designs of leger lead is also good for this purpose. I refer, of course, to the 'coffin lead'. But I do not care for it in it's original form which allows for the line to be passed through the whole length of the lead. It is much better to put a swivel in at one end and gently tap the lead round it to make it a fixture. The line can then be passed through the swivel and the whole rig will be more sensitive to bites. Bored round bullets can be treated similarly but they are of little use where the lead has to remain stationary. They are better employed for the rolling techniques.

All the above-mentioned leger leads are stopped from sliding down the line by split shot pinched on at a pre-determined distance from the hook. This distance between lead and hook can be of the utmost importance and is usually referred to as the 'link'. It is up to the angler to decide what length it shall be. Where the water is still or slow, for instance, a bait lying on the bottom will not be unduly disturbed by currents. Therefore baits such as paste, worms, maggots, etc., may lie at rest a yard or even more from the leger lead.

But in fast water it may be necessary to put the stop shot a lot nearer so that the bait does not rise too high or wave about too much in the current. When the bait is crust, which is very buoyant, it may be necessary to stop the lead only 2 inches from the hook. It depends entirely where the angler wants the bait to fish. There are times when it is advisable to *allow* the bait to waver in the current. Where a steady stream of groundbait has been passing through the swim, for instance, the fish will have become accustomed to baits moving up and down in the undercurrents. In these circumstances a long-link leger, allowing plenty of movement, will probably prove more acceptable than a short one. Where the fish are expected to hug the bottom (chub in very cold weather, for instance), the short-link leger will be the better choice.

It will be seen from this that each angling situation may demand a completely different terminal tackle and knowledge of them is essential for successful legering. Meanwhile *confidence* in legering as a method and *correct use* of the simple terminals described above will, I'm sure, help to put better specimens on the bank.

# 5 The Fixed-Spool Reel

It is doubtful if any other piece of angling equipment has ever come in for as much abuse, or caused as much controversy as the fixed-spool reel. Nor has anything ever been so misused by so many people, despite the fact that thousands of words, diagrams and photographs have been printed to explain its simple function.

In order to try to explain the uses of the fixed-spool reel, it may be necessary to list the number of ways in which it is so readily *misused*. If we can avoid misusing it, we may end up by using it correctly!

First of all, however, let us all accept that the fixed-spool reel is the most versatile reel in use today. In its many sizes there's scarcely a branch of angling that is unsuited to it, despite the fact that it was originally designed for trout spinning with ultra-light baits and very fine lines. Modern fixed-spool reels, though still used for this purpose, have many other functions. They will perform many duties if they are used correctly – but this does not always happen. Let us look at some of the things that go wrong from time to time.

**Filling the spool**

First of all there is the question of filling the spool, so often regarded as unimportant by experienced and inexperienced anglers alike. It is essential that the spool be filled correctly (and filled to within about a sixteenth of an inch of the lip is about right) but quite often this is governed completely by the amount of line the angler buys to put on it. More often than not he buys 100 yards at a time, and, while 100 yards is adequate if used with some cheap backing, it will only half fill some spools used alone. I can only generalize here, of course, because the type of spools and the thickness of the line affect the issue considerably. But whatever you use you *must* fill your reel to the rim less one-sixteenth of an inch (*Figure 9*).

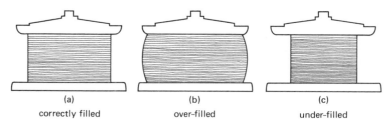

| (a) | (b) | (c) |
|---|---|---|
| correctly filled | over-filled | under-filled |

*Figure 9*

An under-filled spool will result in very poor casting. The distance achieved will be short and inconsistent and there will be little pleasure derived from using it. On the other hand an over-filled spool will cause trouble. Coils of line will fall off at the wrong time and result in the most unpleasant 'bird's nest'. The first lesson we must learn, then, is to fill the spool correctly, and this is easily done if we have two identical spools.

Let us assume that we have 100 yards of line and need backing to build it up so that the spool is correctly filled. First we wind the 100 yards of line *directly on* to the first spool and we *top it* up with backing to the required height. Then we simply transfer it all *en bloc* to the second spool and it cannot be other than correctly filled!

## Casting

Moving on to the casting, let us look at a few faults usually incurred in this operation.

First there are the side-swipers and swishers who are anything but accurate in their casting. They are inaccurate simply because they *are* side-swipers. If you swing sideways with your rod you cannot always be accurate, even though you may have had years of experience. The eventual path of the lure or bait is decided by the moment at which you release the reel line.

A fraction of a second either way will put you well off course.

If, on the other hand, you use an overhead or underhand swing so that the rod is pointing towards your target you will at least be accurate with regard to direction if not for distance.

In other words you may drop short of where you're aiming or you may shoot over the top but you'll never drop to the left or right.

The forefinger of the reel hand controls the line while the bale arm is open.

It is entirely wrong to hold the line between thumb and forefinger of the *left* hand while you cast with the *right*. This results in the line wrapping itself round the handle or the reel stem as well as inaccurate casting.

## Fishing

So we come to using the reel to fish with, as distinct from playing a fish. The greater part of coarse fishing is practised from one point, and in many instances it is simply a question of casting and waiting for a bite. In still waters when deadbaiting for pike or fishing for carp the bale arm is left open to allow for free movement of the line when a fish takes the bait.

When legering in rivers, the bale arm is usually closed and the bite registered on the rod tip. Long trotting may be practised very efficiently with the fixed-spool reel, especially if it is a modern one with a fast retrieve. As the float goes on its way downstream, the finger controls the line as it comes off the spool in loops while the bale arm remains open. When a strike is made following a bite, the finger traps the line against the spool and holds the fish until the bale arm is snapped home. A little practice is required here, but it is soon mastered. Trotting with a fixed-spool reel can be as pleasant and as effective as it is with a centre pin once these simple operations are understood.

Spinning is a more active form of fishing and is more popular than ever today because the fixed-spool reel is available to everyone at a reasonable price. But because casting with a fixed-spool reel is remarkably easy, there is a tendency among many anglers to behave like automatons – cast, retrieve, cast, retrieve – unthinkingly and, invariably, in too much of a hurry. There is a tendency, too, to cast exceptionally long distances and then, it seems, to wind the lure back as quickly as possible in order to cast again. Once again I have to generalize, but I believe it is much better to search thinkingly and with short casts retrieved as slowly as conditions allow. Vary the speed and direction of the retrieve and use the current wherever possible.

## Playing the fish

Finally we come to the important question of playing fish on the fixed-spool reel. Too many people believe (and too many so-called experts advise) that it is only necessary to set the clutch so that it slips under stress and that it only remains to keep winding until the fish is on the bank!

The technique of playing a fish on a fixed-spool reel has to be learned — and it needs practice to learn it properly. Nevertheless it is not a difficult technique if a few elementary points are studied.

The first and most important lesson to learn is NOT to wind against a fish taking line. If you have to put pressure on a fish, do it by placing a finger on the spool and pressing against it.

The second lesson to learn is the art of pumping. This is essential when you need to retrieve against a strong fish. Briefly, the rod point is lowered slowly, and contact maintained with the fish by winding at the same time. Then the rod is raised strongly so that the fish comes with it (finger on the spool all the time, giving no line, but ready to release it the moment the fish makes a powerful move) and the process is repeated as often as is necessary to bring the fish to net.

Learn these two points, and you will never suffer from line kink or from the weakness it eventually causes. Learn to clamp down on a fish with finger pressure and to release it when necessary and you'll lose very few fish and suffer very few breakages.

# 6 Weed Removal and Fishery Management

Back in the 1950s *Angling Times* featured my brothers and me catching tench at Wotton Lakes. Quite a lot was written about our methods and one particular paragraph told the readers: 'The Taylor. brothers believe that to catch fish means lots of hard work beforehand, but they know that it is time and labour well spent. The excellent fishing they have enjoyed is ample proof.' How true these words are, and although they referred at the time to tench, the catching of specimen fish of any kind will be assured if you are prepared to put in some spade-work beforehand. Spade-work does not necessarily mean the removal of weeds to make swims fishable, neither does it mean the cutting down of trees, bushes and bank herbage to make swims accessible.

The removal of weeds and bank obstruction is often necessary but there are many times when it would be better to plant new ones. I have, many times, seen overhanging willows, beautiful chub lies, ruthlessly cut down to 'make the swim fishable'. The fact that when the willows went the chub went also, did not appear to matter as long as the anglers(?) concerned could cast without being snagged.

The same applies to many beautiful stretches of river. I have seen them stripped of their weed growth and consequently their insect life for hundreds of yards at a time. I was guilty many years ago of a similar action and it took five years for that particular stretch to recover. Luckily I was able to convince the other members of the syndicate that the strange disappearance of our roach from that spot was our own fault and it was left unmolested from then on.

Since then I have been very wary about removing weed from the river in too large a quantity, and rather than cut down trees, I have been at great pains to plant new ones during the months of April and May. Planting willows and sallow bushes is a simple job, but one that repays in a few years' time. All you have to do is to cut some branches off a living willow or sallow and push them into the wet ground at the water's edge. A walk along the river studying the set of the current will soon give you an idea of where they will prove most effective and in a few years' time you'll be glad that you encouraged those big chub to stay.

All this may sound good advice to those who rent their own fishery, but members of clubs will probably have difficulty in convincing the majority of its wisdom. It seems that a great many club members are more concerned about losing a few sixpenny hooks than they are about their failure to catch fish. It is usually these people who propose 'that such and such an obstruction shall be removed', and having seen the resolution passed, are content to sit back and let 'the old faithfuls' of the working party do the removing. The 'old faithfuls' do it against their better judgement, but they have little choice. It is up to all of us to attend our meetings and oppose these resolutions when we are convinced that they are detrimental to the fishery. Too many banks have been spoiled by thoughtless anglers!

However, in spite of all this, there are many places, especially in still waters, where weed clearance is essential. It is not much use knowing the whereabouts of large tench or carp if they are in weed beds too thick to get a bait into. Shallow lakes breed good-quality fish as a rule, because of their luxurious weed growth, but often, in order to catch these fish, some of the weed has to be removed. Generally speaking it is impossible to remove too much weed from shallow lakes without mechanical means, so that there is not much fear of overdoing it. Swim clearance is hard work and we have never had any worries about removing too much weed – our trouble is in removing enough!

Quite often you can save yourself a lot of work on a tench swim merely by baiting it regularly for about three weeks before the season opens. Where the weed is not too thick to prevent the groundbait from reaching the bottom you will find that the tench themselves will do 90 per cent of the work for you. Tench are great weed-shifters. Where weed is thick, however, the only answer is tools and hard work. If you are a lone hand you will have to carry a small drag and/or cutter, light enough to throw out and retrieve single handed for a whole day if necessary.

One excellent tool for cutting lilies and rushes was devised by Richard Walker and publicized in the *Angling Times*. It is light and portable and it is easy to handle. When it is thrown out and retrieved in a series of jerks, those lily stalks and bulrushes fairly pop out of the

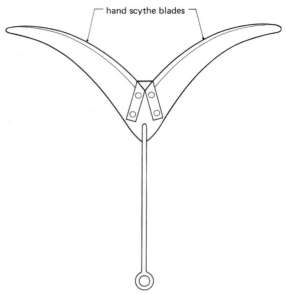

hand scythe blades

*Figure 10*    One-man cutter, devised by Richard Walker

water. It can be made for a few shillings and should be in the bottom of every angler's bag. With one of these and a small two-sided rake, two men can clear many square yards of weed-choked water in a few hours (*Figure 10*).

Another excellent tool devised by Richard Walker and Maurice Ingham, specifically for use at Redmire, is a light chain cutter. It is comprised of about 15 yards of lavatory chain (Woolworths), two cylindrical weights of about 4 pounds each and two 50-yard lengths of rope. It is assembled in the order – rope, weight, chain, weight, rope – and it is used from a punt (*Figure 11*). The end of the first rope is tied to the bank and the rest of the tackle is rowed out for its whole 50 yards. The first weight is then dropped overboard and the boat turned at right angles parallel to the bank while the chain is paid out. The second weight is then dropped overboard and the boat turned again towards the bank, meanwhile paying out the second length of rope. The two rope ends should now be about 15 yards apart, i.e. the length of the chain, and the pulling operation takes place from those two points. The two operators must work together, pulling slowly and smoothly at the same time. If the operation is carried out properly an area of 15 yards by 50 yards is cleared of weed in one sweep! Huge

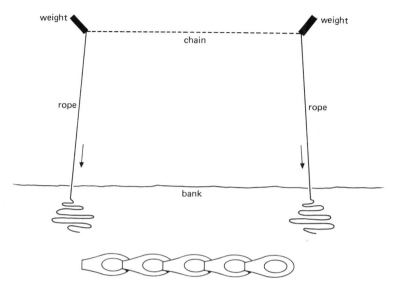

*Figure 11*    Ingham/Walker chain cutter in action

carpets of weed come to the surface and drift away, and as a rule there is no need to repeat the operation. It just has to be seen to be believed! I should point out here that this equipment is not very successful in water less than 6 feet deep as the chain tends to slide over the weed rather than cut it. In water between 6 and 12 feet deep though, it cuts through weed like a knife through butter. The secret lies in taking your time. Coil the equipment neatly on the boat and pay it out carefully making sure that the chain is not kinked as it goes overboard. Get the weights and chain down to the bottom in the right place and pull it back slowly.

With extra long ropes and a little manipulation this equipment can be used from the bank even when a punt is not available. Wide corners can be cleared and areas a considerable way from the bank can be dealt with, provided the ropes are long enough to allow the tackle to span the lake completely. The tackle is walked into position by one operator, who carries one rope end around to the far side of the lake and pulls the weights and chain into the desired position. The two operators then move in to a distance of 15 yards and retrieve as before.

My brothers and I do most of our tench-fishing in water no more than 3 feet deep, especially at the beginning of the season. The weed beds in these spots are so dense that we have to clear very large areas before it is possible to fish at all. The tackle so far described is inadequate for such major operations and in order to beat the weed problem we have to take drastic measures. It is a filthy job and usually involves several weekends of hard work.

We use, for these operations, a drag some six or seven feet long and weighing about 60 pounds. Ours was made by a club member out of a length of heavy-gauge barrel tubing and it fairly bristles with spikes. It is a formidable tool, requiring little but brute strength to use, but it removes weed by the hundredweight! The original method used by club members was to tow it out on a boat for some 20 yards and then retrieve it from the bank, but my brothers and I use it with two ropes

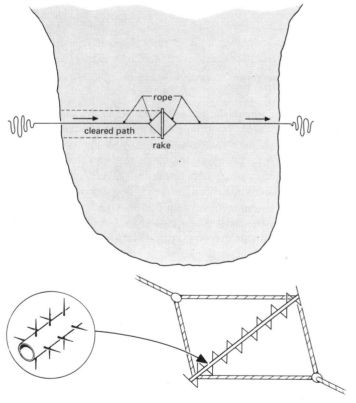

*Figure 12*   Heavy metal drag for drastic weed clearance

and 'see-saw' it from point to point. We have to co-opt a fourth member to help in these operations (*Figure 12*). Sometimes we use it from bank to bank across wide corners and sometimes completely across the lake. At others we use it between two boats or between one boat and the bank.

Some years ago we cleared an area of 100 yards long by 80 yards wide with this tool, long ropes and assistance from several members of the Vale of Aylesbury AA. We heaved it back and forth across the narrow end of the Warrells lake at Wotton, removing about $1\frac{1}{2}$ hundredweight of weed at each sweep. Every second sweep we moved another foot along the bank and by the beginning of the season there was scarcely a weed left at that end of the lake. The weed situation had become so serious that an action such as this had to be taken and on the whole sport improved. Members were then able to leger at a range of 50 yards which had previously been impossible.

Whichever way you use a tool such as this you will find it exhausting work but using it from two boats requires a lot of preparation beforehand. It is essential to get the boats firmly fixed in the correct positions before operations begin, otherwise you will find yourselves swearing as well as sweating. Drive into the mud four strong stakes (one at each 'corner') to each boat, and tie the boats securely. If you do not do this you will find that the drag stays put and you'll pull the boats along when you start 'see-sawing'. In any case the stakes will soon work loose, and you will find that they need constant attention. In water over about 5 feet in depth the leverage on the stakes becomes too great and this method is not successful. In depths of 3 or 4 feet however it is ideal. We usually clear an area some-what larger than we require and deposit the weed at the extreme ends after removal. It sinks to the bottom and is therefore not actually removed from the lake altogether. At times, when the weather is favourable, we don swimsuits and work in these, taking turns actually in the water removing the weed from the drag. This saves a lot of effort in that the drag does not have to be lifted clear of the water each time. It is somewhat easier on clothes and also serves to keep us cool whilst doing a very hot and tiresome job. We usually end up by diving overboard and inspecting the swim at close quarters to see if any weed remains. All this may sound a little drastic and of course it's not everyone's 'cup of tea' but we find it enjoyable in more than one respect. In conjunction with sensible pre-baiting it has often brought bags of forty, fifty, sixty and even seventy-odd tench to our nets in a single day. Today, I have lost count of the numbers of 4 and 5 pound tench we have caught but it must run into thousands.

To repeat the words of *Angling Times* – we consider it time and labour well spent.

# 7 Chub

The chub has been described as 'the fearfullest of fishes' and, having many times watched chub do their famous disappearing act in face of danger, I can but admit that the description is a very apt one.

However, the chub is also a very obliging fish. Conditions are seldom so bad that he will not feed at some time of the day in some place or other along the river. I do not know of a fish which will greedily accept such a vast number of baits as the chub. Except perhaps on very hard-fished waters the chub is not a tackle-conscious fish and there is no need to fish for him with fine tackle. He is however, very 'angler conscious', and the whole basis of success in chub fishing is to find your chub, without him first finding you. Provided the angler remains out of sight of the fish, and does not wield his rod in full view of him, he will catch chub. The type of bait he is using at the time is of relative unimportance under most conditions. It should, however, be a good-sized mouthful.

There are times when a smaller bait is successful of course, and I will go into the question of small baits later in this chapter.

If I tried to list the baits which have been successful in tempting chub of all sizes I should need a couple of pages in which to do so, and then I have no doubt I should miss plenty of them out. However, here are a few baits which I *know* to have been successful: worms, cheese and cheese paste, bread flake, crust, suet, that old favourite pith and brains, green peas, maggots, crayfish, frogs, sausage, minnows (live, or spun as deadbait), spoons, plugs, spinners, cherries, elderberries, newts, grasshoppers, daddy longlegs, caterpillars, bluebottles, artificial flies (wet or dry), cabbage butterflies, white moths and a host of others. Of these, I do not think that for *all-round* conditions there is one to beat the first named – lobworms, followed by crust and cheese in that order. There is perhaps one instance where this rule does not apply and that is on a river which holds a head of crayfish. In summer chub cannot resist crayfish either whole or in part – but the angler must still remain out of sight all the time.

There are two distinct types of chub-fishing. One consists of sending a bait in search of chub, the angler, meanwhile remaining out of sight upstream. The other consists of first finding the chub and casting a bait to it. The former is almost a necessity on the larger rivers. It is skilful and productive but it is not half so exciting as the latter, which is practically the only method to employ on the smaller, more intimate waters. There is a great satisfaction to be gained from finding a chub, being sure that he is unaware of your presence, casting accurately to him and *watching* him take the bait.

With the first-mentioned method there is little change needed for summer or winter fishing. The chub will be found in different haunts of course but the method used to catch them is much the same.

With the second method there is some difference in tactics and approach between summer and winter fishing.

I know of no type of fishing where a float is less necessary than with chub fishing. Trotting for chub with a shotted float is quite delightful, but a roving leger, though perhaps not so productive, will on the whole take the larger fish. For the rest of this discourse on chub fishing I shall have no more to say with regard to floats. They are usually unnecessary and there is no point in encumbering the line with unnecessary articles of tackle.

Let us deal first with the larger waters where it is necessary to send a bait in search of the chub. Having decided on the swim to be fished and the bait to be used, the angler should get well upstream of it – tackle up and get down as low as possible. In doing so he will of course scare the daylights out of a number of fish, but it is better to do this than to remain perched up on the skyline in full view of the fish *all* the time. Some experiment will be necessary before the right size of lead is found and my idea of the ideal tackle for this kind of fishing is as follows.

A two-piece 10 foot or a three-piece 11 foot Avon-type rod set up leger style, with a leger lead of just sufficient weight to hold the stream, stopped by one shot about 3 feet from the hook. Line strength depending on conditions can be up to 6 pounds breaking strain and hook size may vary from size 10 to size 6, depending on the bait to be used. On very fast waters, such as the Hampshire Avon, it is the practice of the experts to leave as much as 5 feet between lead and hook. The bait is cast across the stream and the rod placed in the rest until the line tightens as the lead is carried downstream. After a few seconds' pause, the rod point is lifted and a little more line paid out. A further pause and the procedure is repeated at intervals until the bait is some thirty yards downstream. At this point it can be left considerably longer until it is eventually retrieved and cast again. A wide area can be searched using this method by varying the distance or direction of the cast. The bait can be held hard in the likeliest spots before being allowed to go on its way again. If the rod point is lifted *without* allowing more line to be taken the bait will eventually finish up under the angler's own bank some short distance downstream. Do not neglect your own bank when fishing in this manner! Many good chub lie under the near bank and are overlooked or scared to death by thoughtless anglers.

When chub take the bait, there is no mistaking it as a rule, especially if the bait is a big one. There are occasions when they can be a bit 'finicky', but conditions usually point to this and the angler can fish accordingly. Very often, the bait will be taken when it is on the move; the chub will grab it in passing and will have no time to be 'finicky'.

Groundbait of a fairly stiff consistency, and containing samples of the hookbait, should be thrown upstream periodically so that particles of it are continuously passing through the swim.

If you should hook a large chub and you are doubtful about bringing it twenty or thirty yards upstream against the current you can nip smartly downstream and get below it. It is easier to beat a fish from downstream and not so hard on the tackle. Inevitably you will lose a chub, and for a time this will put paid to your fishing, but the loss of a fish will not put them off nearly so much as the sight of someone walking the banks. If you lose a fish, do not go for a walk afterwards! Stay put and groundbait a little heavier for a while. Chub *will* come back once they are assured that danger is past.

In extremely cold conditions, a small bait is more likely to be successful than a large one. The chub must still be searched for, but it is policy to search for them more slowly. Let your bait travel shorter distances at a time and leave it static for considerably longer periods. Chub, although willing to feed under cold conditions, do not bite so boldly. They will take a small bait quite delicately, more often than not when it is stationary, and the angler's reactions to these delicate bites must be quick.

Chub on the smaller rivers need a different approach and different

techniques, and although the fish are more likely to see the angler and be thoroughly scared, he can often turn this to his own advantage at a later date. Chub-fishing on small weed-choked rivers is an intimate affair and the angler meets his quarry at very close quarters – sometimes under his very rod tip. It is an exhausting business in the summer, and means a lot of crawling along banks, peering over rush beds and casting among thick vegetation. In the summer though, the fact that the bank vegetation is high is often an advantage as it can be used as a screen. It hampers one's casting, of course, and, as one only has one chance as a rule, a muffed cast means a move on to the next likely spot. If you try this type of fishing you will get drenched with early morning dew, you will be stung by nettles and thorns and you will perspire. The moment you perspire you will be the centre of attraction for every fly, midge and mosquito along the river. You may at that moment be watching a chub, waiting the chance to throw a bait to him, so you will not be able to brush away those flies, midges or mosquitoes. If you do, it is quite likely that the movement of your hand will put him down, so you will have to suffer them in silence. What happens when you see your chance? Of course you miss! These flies, midges and mosquitoes have affected your nerves and your temper to such an extent that your aim is terrible, and instead of the bait landing in the vicinity of the chub, it lands in the bushes on the far bank. That, briefly, is chub chasing in the summer; but of course it is not always as bad as that.

During your walks along the small river you will get to know the haunts of chub, and if you cannot see them on the day you are trying to catch them just drop your bait in the places where you *have* seen them and search about for them. For this type of fishing you will need sturdy tackle in view of the conditions. It is hard to say what strength is the best – I seldom use less than 6 pounds breaking strain monofilament and I have been smashed in a most devastating manner using 10 pounds breaking strain. There is no need for anything else on the line except a hook and a bait. A fixed-spool reel is, I should say, essential for this type of casting – and I am almost inclined to say that the bigger the bait the better it is. On the whole I think a big lobworm is the best bait and if you think that you need extra weight in order to reach your fish when you cast – *don't* start piling lead on to the line. Put another lobworm on your hook and if that isn't heavy enough –

Ken Taylor with a big chub—back in the good old days!

put another one on. Don't worry about it being too large a mouthful – it can't be for summer chub fishing!

Sometimes the 'take' will be seen. A pair of large lips will open up and engulf the worm before it has had time to move more than a few inches. Other times the line will be seen to cut across the water as the chub turns with its prize. The importance of 'keeping in touch' with the bait cannot be too strongly stressed as the fish has to be stopped dead in its tracks, held hard and brought to net all in one continuous movement. There is no question of playing the fish, in fact, give it an inch and it will play you! Breaks are fewer than one would think but some fish are bound to come adrift, and many will succeed in reaching the rushes and force you to pull for a break.

Perhaps the best kind of 'take' is the one that is felt on the rod point. Chub in the small rivers, the same as chub in most places, take big baits with a bang, and if you *feel* the bite you will have a good chance of gaining control of the fish in the shortest space of time.

At times you may find a shoal of chub in full view of you and they will all vary in size. The problem is how to offer a suitable bait to the largest or near-largest one. I have never succeeded in doing it! Somehow it is always one of the smaller ones which gets there first. I suppose that is how the biggest one got so big!

The need for camouflage was brought home to me once when I took a comparative novice with me on to one of the smaller rivers. He was not content to wear sombre clothes, but adorned his hat with rush-stems and smeared his face with mud. He caught three chub all bigger than my brace – and now I wear a special camouflaged hat, with brown and green strings hanging over my face for 'chub chasing'! Other baits are often just as successful as lobworms and if there are crayfish present in the river, they can be used as bait with deadly effect, either whole or just the tail end. A large hook is essential, and I use a No. 2 carp hook and place it in between the last two tail segments. A little time should be allowed before striking to ensure that the hook is in the chub's mouth and a very firm strike is necessary to drive these large hooks home. A crayfish has one distinct advantage over other baits in that it stays on the hook longer and is almost snag-proof, due to its tough outer shell.

A dead frog cast slightly downstream and retrieved in a series of jerks is another deadly summer bait for chub.

Fly-fishing using the usual big buzzy flies is rather difficult except in the more open water, but it will often catch the smaller chub. You will quite possibly hook big ones too and I hope you land them — but I find, on the waters I fish, that the normal dry-fly outfit is not powerful enough to stop a large chub from reaching his favourite snag. I find also that even the most modern fly reel has a very feeble rate of line recovery and on small overgrown rivers, speed of recovery is very important.

It is not always possible to approach the water without being seen or causing some disturbance and very often the reeds and rushes have to be broken down before you can get a bait into the water at all. When this is necessary the only thing to do is to settle down, concealed and comfortable, and wait for the fish to reappear. You can throw out your bait first if you like but I think it is better to wait until you see the fish again before you do so.

There are times when a chub cannot resist a bait which is dropped in front of or behind it. It takes it in a flash, whereas it will often ignore a bait which remains still on the bottom.

At the end of the summer I find that chub-fishing 'goes off' a bit. There seems to be a 'dead spot' somewhere about the middle of September. The leaves of some of the trees have already started to fall and the chub cannot be seen so often or so well as they were at the height of the summer. It is, however, a little too early to commence orthodox winter-style fishing for them and although I have tried various methods in all the usual swims I have not had much success until the first frosts have arrived.

I think that it is better to pursue each species of fish during the season when you know them to be more likely to feed and so, after several years of September chub fishing, I find that it pays me to give them a rest for a month or so and seek the roach and perch instead. I am still referring to my local small rivers here. September can be a good month for Avon, Stour and Thames chub.

However, once the 'dead spot' has passed and the greenery is rapidly turning brown, I return to the chub as my main quarry on the river. Perhaps by that time the first floods have come and gone and the river has enjoyed its first flush out. I find then that the chub are not very far from their summer haunts — not in the exact spots perhaps, but not many yards away.

Disregarding water temperature for a bit I think that if you can find a flow of current equal to that in which you saw your chub in summer — that is where you will find them in winter. Places which were dead slack in summer will have a little more 'stream' in October and those parts which held the chub in summer will by then be moving a little too fast for the chub to remain there. Go to your old summer chub swim – study the current and try to find the nearest spots to it, which are now moving about as fast as the chub swim did in summer. Chub do not move far – but they will move into a *comfortable stream* from one which is moving too fast for them. Except in time of high flood they seldom move into the really dead slack water. It has often been advocated that chub be sought in the deeper water once the winter has set in. The old theory was that the deeper water was the warmer water, but it isn't! River water is always on the move and the temperature is likely to be the same in two feet of water as in ten feet. I do not say that you will not find chub in deeper water. You will, of course, as the deeper water is often the water with the most comfortable current. However, that does not mean that chub will not be found in the shallows. Some of my best chub have been taken from 2 feet of water in extremely cold weather, and don't forget that chub can probably see *you* better in *deep* water than they can in shallow. This may not appear correct but it is a fact.

For winter chub-fishing on the smaller rivers the same tackle can be employed as described earlier for large river chub. You will be much closer to your fish than you would be on the large river, but you will be able to fish at a slightly longer range than you did in summer, as much of the plant life will have been swept away. You will not be able to search so widely for your fish and it will pay you to leave the bait static for considerable periods. Under the bushes on the far bank there will accumulate a wealth of rush, reeds and rubbish. Cast as near to it as you dare with your leger tackle and watch the rod tip. If the water temperature is over 40°F. you can stick to lobworms, but as it drops below that you will probably be more successful with cheese or flake. When the water temperature reaches as low as 38°F. then I think you will be more successful with crust – and it does not have to be a large cube, a $\frac{3}{8}$ in. cube is large enough. As this is virtually a static type of fishing, the bait must be kept from wavering about in the current. It must be on, or very near, the bottom so the best type of rig is a leger with the weight stopped a mere 2 inches from the hook. Chub will move very slowly under these cold conditions and that in itself is the secret of the static leger. They are averse to snapping up a bait that swims past them, but they can sidle up to a static bait and suck it in as slowly as they like. Consequently these bites are finicky – and you must be ready to strike at the merest flicker of your rod tip.

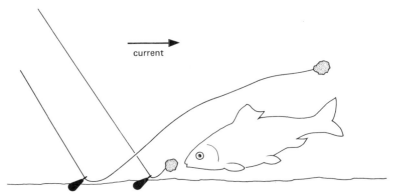

*Figure 13*   Chub or roach hugging the bottom in cold water may overlook a bait fished on a long link leger tackle

Occasionally you may pick up a roach, but they do not normally frequent chub swims. If you find that your favourite chub swim produces only small roach and dace you can move on to pastures new – it is doubtful if the chub will be there on that day. As likely as not, if you look you will see that the river has dropped or risen a couple of inches or so – and this can make a vast difference to the chub's whereabouts. The level of the river has a definite effect on the current and chub insist on a comfortable current!

That is the difference between the larger rivers and the smaller ones. Every few yards or so the smaller rivers change in depth, current and character and they become easier to understand than wide reaches of uniform depth. Chub do not have to move long distances upstream or downstream to find a suitable environment; a mere rod's length is often far enough. Groundbaiting on the whole is unnecessary. If your choice of swim is a wrong one, groundbait will not often induce chub into it, but a few hookbait samples thrown into it may tempt the chub to move around in search of more if your choice is a right one.

Above all when fishing for chub – keep down – keep quiet – keep still – and don't neglect the water under your own bank.

Chub can be caught from some rivers in summer and autumn on floating crusts. Many years ago it was recognized as a very effective way of catching Hampshire Avon fish, and there were odd times when barbel could be caught that way too. It is, perhaps, not generally known that the method works very well in winter on some waters. It's a fact that, for much of the time, chub tend to lie deep in the cold water of winter, but they *will* come to the surface if the attraction is strong enough. A steady stream of floating crusts, covering an area where chub are known to shoal, will often start things moving. Even in really cold conditions, chub can sometimes be tempted towards the surface, and it would appear that they are encouraged to do so more readily on bright days. They react to sunshine and will often feed on the surface in sunny conditions despite low water temperature.

Some years ago a Great Ouse chub weighing over 6 pounds was reported taken by a schoolboy using floating breadcrust, and on one memorable occasion chub were seen to take crusts in a hole in the ice. Finding chub isn't always easy, but here's a little wrinkle to consider.

Dace are well known for the way they behave in sunny conditions and most anglers are aware that they can often be located in fairly shallow water by scattering a few handfuls of casters at the head of a streamy run. If dace *are* present they will show themselves almost immediately by swirling at the drifting baits. At first you don't see them. The bottom is clearly visible but somehow the fish remain hidden or completely camouflaged for as long as they remain still. Only when they move to intercept the floating food do they come into view. Then their shadowy forms and occasional, silvery flashes as they turn in the stream show up perfectly. And where the dace revel in the shallows there's always a chance that chub are not too far away. I have seen them lying at the tail end of the run, quietly sucking in baits the dace have missed, and I have fed them steadily and weaned them over to small crust cubes before sending down a hook similarly baited. Sometimes I've been lucky, sometimes the slight difference between the hookbait and the free offerings has been duly noted by the chub with the result that they have dropped back downstream, out of sight and no longer interested.

It's difficult to make a hooked crust travel in *exactly* the same way as an unattached portion, but if you can do it, you'll enjoy an exciting form of winter fishing every once in a while. But don't waste too much time trying to catch fish on the surface unless it's really on. Most times you'll do better with an orthodox leger or float tackle, but it *is* a pleasant change occasionally to do something that's not usually reckoned to be in the book.

# 8 Tench

It ought not to be necessary to describe the tench, for there can be few anglers who have not seen one at some time or other. The small red eye, the large pelvic fins, the smooth and beautifully proportioned body and the olive-green colouring are a combination of characteristics which only the tench can claim. Despite this, however, I have known occasions when a very moderate leather carp has been mistaken for a large tench and therefore a brief description is perhaps excusable here.

It is my opinion that the only British freshwater fish likely to be confused with the tench is a leather carp, and for the purposes of recognition, it is only necessary to remember that, while the leather carp is virtually scaleless, the tench is evenly covered with small scales. The tench also has only two barbules compared with the leather carp which has four. Colour variations arise from water to water and apart from the olive-green coloration already mentioned the tench can also be buff or almost black, depending mainly on environment.

Tench are mainly lovers of still or slow-moving waters and, while they are reputed to prefer the mud-bottomed reaches, there are many waters with hard and stony bases which breed tench of enormous size. Where a choice of both types of bottom is available the tench seem to show no particular preference. They are equally at home among the bulrushes in the gravel as they are among the weeds in the mud.

In May or early June they emerge from a long winter's sojourn on or in the lake bottom and may be seen rolling and splashing in the weedy shallows at this time. Sometimes this rolling is a preliminary to the spawning act; sometimes the spawning does not take place until the coarse-fishing season is well under way. I have yet to catch a tench during the first week of the season which I could confidently say had finished spawning, and I have seen them performing these duties as late as August.

Tench are truly summer fish and remain very active during the warmer months, but retire to the bottom and remain more or less torpid as soon as the first frosts arrive. It is said that they bury themselves in the mud but, while I agree that they are capable of burying themselves, I do not believe that all tench do so. Neither do I believe that they retire to the deeper water before settling down for the winter as is commonly supposed. I have watched for the first appearance of tench for a number of years and in the waters where I have studied them they invariably show themselves first in the shallow weedy water. It is my opinion that, rather than set about burying themselves in the deeps, some tench, at least, move into the thick weed at the first signs of approaching cold weather, and let the weed die naturally around them. In this way they are, to all intents and purposes, buried and having retired to the shallows for the winter, it is logical to expect them to reappear there in the spring. In fact this is exactly what often happens. This theory is somewhat substantiated by the fact that very often many more late-season tench are caught in the shallower water than in the deeps. I believe that tench move to the deeper water at the height of the summer at such times as when the water is very warm. Undoubtedly tench like warm water but when they are in it they seldom feed. When the sun is bright they will laze and occasionally roll on the surface of the shallow water, but it is usually in the deeper and comparatively cooler water that they feed. I am referring here to the tench population of waters of average depth with a choice of both shallows and deeps. In large deep flooded gravel pits, a depth of around 12 feet would be considered shallow; in the average tench lake, canal or slow moving river it would probably be the maximum depth. It is hard to say what constitutes the shallows of a deep gravel pit and the behaviour of tench in these waters is different and somewhat difficult to understand. Often gravel pits are fairly weed-free and do not offer suitable spawning media for the tench. But the tench make use of whatever shallow water is available in which to spawn and the pattern is very similar in most waters at this time. Tench in deep pits are not affected so much by the prevailing conditions after spawning, and this often makes them difficult to locate. They may rove for several weeks quite near to the surface without feeding in the accepted place, i.e. the bottom. This makes their capture considerably more difficult than the tench in shallower waters, but eventually they settle in areas where the water is not extremely deep and commence feeding on the bottom. It may be that the water in these pits is very much cooler (except near to the surface) at this time of year and that it takes some weeks for the bottom to warm up. In the extreme deeps, of course, the water remains cool, but in depths of 12 to 15 feet (the depth at which many tench establish themselves in deep gravel pits) the water probably remains at a fairly comfortable temperature once it has warmed up. I have never taken any extensive temperature readings in deep gravel pits; my efforts in this field have been confined to shallow lakes, but I cannot recall the capture of any tench from the extreme depths of large gravel pits.

Tench in large, deep reservoirs follow a similar pattern and are seldom caught early in the season, except in comparatively shallow water.

In canals of fairly even depth the location of tench is mainly a matter of food supply. Depth and temperature do not vary much from one stretch to another, and the fish could be anywhere at a given time. Some areas, however, become established as tench haunts and, while there is no apparent reason for this, it is probably due to the amount of natural food available. Where the canals are navigable there appears to be a tendency for the tench to settle in the vicinity of wide bends with vertical banks. The constant washing of the banks by passing barge traffic undoubtedly releases a lot of natural food and many tench are caught from near bank swims in these areas.

As with all other species of fish, there are waters which breed tench of enormous size, waters which breed many tench of a very high average size and waters where the tench seldom reach a weight of more than $1\frac{1}{2}$ pounds. The latter are usually described as 'hungry waters' which offer ideal spawning facilities for the tench, but very little in the way of natural food to maintain a good growth rate. Invariably the tench in these waters are easy to catch and, as the numbers increase a very low average weight level is established and the strain becomes stunted.

**Feeding habits**

Broadly speaking the tench waters of this country can be divided into two categories: soft-bottomed waters and hard-bottomed waters. The tench in both types of waters are, in the main, bottom feeders and spend a great deal of their time grubbing around for food on the bottom of the lake or river. Their feeding habits differ somewhat, however, in that the tench in soft-bottomed waters tend to dig deeply in the mud, whereas those in hard-bottomed waters do not find the digging so necessary.

In soft-bottomed waters much of the food is composed of small, and often minute, forms of larvae, shrimps, worms, leeches, etc.; in hard-bottomed waters the natural food is composed mainly of snails and molluscs. In both types of water the action of feeding sends bubbles to the surface of the water, but these bubbles are much more pronounced where digging takes place. The water over a soft bottom becomes much more discoloured than that over a clean gravel bottom; the bubbles appear to be smaller but usually cover larger areas.

It would be wrong to suggest that tench are essentially nocturnal in habit but there is no doubt that much of their feeding takes place during the hours of darkness. Much depends upon prevailing conditions, and I have known tench to remain active and in feeding mood day and night for several days in one small area. Usually this occurs during a spell of settled weather, with the water temperature remaining fairly steady day and night. This usually means that the days, though warm, are overcast and the nights are cloudy. Hot days are usually followed by clear, cool nights and tench then often retire to deeper water during the night and again when the sun is at its height.

I consider the ideal water temperature to be somewhere in the lower 60s Fahrenheit, but I think it is more important for the temperature, whatever it is, to remain steady and not fluctuate seriously from day to day. Early morning feeding sessions in very hot weather are a lot shorter in duration and as soon as the sun is strong on the water the tench often become inactive. I have watched them many times swimming idly over a bed of groundbait without showing any inclination to feed. Often they will rise to the surface and hide their heads in the thick weed beds, and only an occasional flick of the tail betrays their presence. At such times it is almost impossible to catch them, but as the sun goes down they often commence feeding on the bottom and continue to do so until the night becomes clear and cold.

All tench do not behave thus, however, and many of them move into the deeper water when the sun is high and feed on through the day. Others retire to the margins and feed in the shade of the reed and rush stems. Often the marginal plants can be seen shuddering violently as the tench move among them searching for food. This is one of several instances when tench do *not* feed on the bottom. They take their food from the stems of the plants and feed at about mid-water. Often the food is dislodged by their moving bodies and taken as it sinks towards the bottom. In these circumstances a bait fished hard on the bottom will not often be successful.

In long-established, soft-bottomed waters a type of feeding often occurs which is nowadays referred to as preoccupied feeding. The items of food are undoubtedly very small and diligent searching by the tench is necessary in order to procure sufficient for their demands. Because of their intense concentration and their preoccupation with one particular type of food, other larger and more easily acquired food is overlooked or ignored by the tench. This often explains the reason why the angler's lobworm or bread bait is not taken, despite the fact that many tench are seen to be active and feeding freely in the swim.

Tench are seldom regarded as being surface feeders and they seldom take any of their natural food from the top, but there are many waters where the tench have learned to take floating food. These waters are usually heavily fished and the floating food usually consists of bread which has been discarded at nightfall by anglers before leaving. The surface feeding often takes place during the night, but I have seen and caught many tench on floating crust baits during the daytime when few fish were feeding on the bottom. I believe that it takes many years for the tench to condition themselves to this type of feeding, but once they have learned to take floating bread, they do so in a most determined manner. I have watched them rise from the deeps and take enormous pieces of crust from under the very noses of several largish carp. Tench-fishing along these lines can often be very exciting and, as with carp-fishing, the presence or otherwise of small rudd gives some indication of their approach. Small rudd and roach seldom remain in the feeding area long after a tench has put in an appearance and this, of course, applies whether the feeding is taking place on the bottom or on the top.

**Tackle**

*Rods*

It has been said that practically any sturdy rod will do for tench-fishing and that one need not be too particular in this respect. For ordinary straightforward float-fishing with such baits as lobworms or paste, where the bites are expected to be slow and deliberate, it is obvious that a quick-striking rod is not necessary. All that is required here is a substantial tool,. having a test curve of about 1 pound, an Avon-type rod (or one of the modern glass equivalents) is, in fact, ideal for the job. It will serve equally well as a leger rod and is capable of dealing with big fish.

In heavily weeded and snaggy waters a slightly more powerful rod may well be considered necessary and, if the leger method is to be employed, there is a lot to be said in favour of a Mark IV carp rod (or one of the modern glass equivalents). It may be considered that such a tool is too powerful and rather unfair on the tench, but I have not found this to be the case. Whenever I have fished the very weedy waters of Wotton Lakes for carp I have used a Mark IV, and while I have yet to catch my first carp from that water, I have caught a large number of tench on this rod. Certainly it is more powerful than the Avon-type rod, but it responds beautifully to the lunges of a hard-fighting tench. I have been thankful for its extra power on more than one occasion and for one whole season I used a Mark IV for all my tench fishing. During the season I took over eighty 4 pounders and seven over 5 pounds. I did not notice that I 'killed' the fish any quicker but there were many fish which I could not have landed on a lighter outfit.

For the greater part of the season, however, I am convinced that more tench will be caught following bites which are delicate or 'finicky' provided they are struck correctly. The numbers of genuine tench bites which are ignored by many anglers and regarded as coming from 'small stuff', amazes me each season. A great majority of these 'touches' undoubtedly come from tench, but are not recognized as tench bites. When they are, they are left to 'develop' but they seldom do. It is here that a quick-striking rod is necessary, but it must also be remembered that the tench is a strong fish. A rod with a tip-only action is virtually useless in dealing with a big tench. It is not made for that type of treatment and it is not fair on the rod. What is required is a fairly fast-striking rod with a good length and action down to the butt.

### Reels

While almost any reel will suffice, there are many circumstances where a fixed-spool reel is necessary with regard to tench-fishing. One thing may be said of all fixed-spool reels and that is that they must be used correctly or their advantages are lost. Long casting is a simple matter, but the art of controlling a fish must be learned; it does not come automatically (see chapter 5, pages 56–7).

## Lines

Generally speaking, the strength of line used is indicated by the water being fished and the size of the fish expected. I have caught tench on lines of 10 pounds breaking strain. I have also caught them on 2 pounds gossamer. I take no credit for catching a large tench on a 2 pound line; I merely considered it necessary because of the conditions in which I was fishing. I do not consider that tench are able to distinguish between heavy lines and fine lines, but undoubtedly there have been occasions when my bait has behaved more naturally at the end of a fine line. It is often necessary to scale everything down considerably in order to present very small baits to shy biting tench, and here the fine line helps considerably.

I would never consider using a fine line simply to achieve the satisfaction of catching a big fish on it. I only use fine lines when I am convinced that I cannot catch the tench otherwise. This does not mean that I advocate cart rope lines for tench-fishing. There is sweet reasonableness in everything and I think that a line of 5 or 6 pounds breaking strain is a very good all-round strength.

## Hooks

Hook size is decided entirely by the size of the bait being used and I can say very little in this respect except to suggest that it is ridiculous to cover a No. 14 with an outsize lobworm, or to impale a grain of wheat on a No. 4. Probably the hook size I use most of all is a No. 10. It will just about accommodate a worm and is suitable for crust, paste, maggots and, at a pinch, wheat. Large baits such as mussels need a No. 4.

I seldom use hooks which are whipped to lengths of gut or nylon but prefer to tie my own direct to the reel line. If my hook comes off through faulty tying I can only blame myself! For this reason I like to use straight-eyed hooks and attach them with a simple half-blood knot. At the end of a day's fishing I throw them away so that there is no risk of using faulty hooks on my next outing. I have seldom found it necessary to sharpen the smaller sizes, but I keep a small stone to touch up the points of the larger ones when I use them.

*Floats*

I have seldom found it necessary to buy expensive floats for tench-fishing. Most of my tench floats are made from peacock quills cut in to five or six lengths according to the size of float required. A foot of model aeroplane fuel tubing will cut up into scores of float caps which fit tightly over the quill. A piece of lead wire will make a simple self-cocker if required.

*Leads and shots*

Generally speaking fancy shotting is unnecessary in tench-fishing and as a rule only one shot is required to cock the float. This can be as large as a swan or as small as a B B, depending on conditions and the bait being fished. An additional or an extra large shot is often necessary for use with stewed wheat baits as I shall explain later.

Where a floatless tackle is indicated there is often no need for lead at all. Such baits as worms, paste and mussels can often be cast without the use of lead but crust cubes, of course, require some weight to keep the bait near the bottom. Often one fixed shot is sufficient, but where long casting is required, an assortment of streamlined swivel leads will be necessary.

I believe in using as little lead as possible in all conditions and if I can get away without using any at all I am happiest.

**Preparations**

Without any doubt at all, successful tench-fishing depends upon the amount of work and preparation one is prepared to do before the actual fishing commences. Most tench waters are extremely weedy, and swims have to be made fishable before the tench can be caught. This means hard work with heavy drags and extensive preparations during the coarse fish close season. Raking on a day-to-day basis during the season proper will also bring results but in order to skim the cream off the June and July tench-fishing it is necessary to begin work much earlier. It has been the policy of my brothers and me to begin our programme towards the end of May (earlier if the weather is suitable) and to ensure that there are feeding tench in the swim at dawn on opening day. I can truthfully say that we have never failed in this respect and that our catches have always been the result of hard work during the close season.

I have explained how best to go about weed clearance in chapter 6 on pages 58–64.

Having chosen a swim and cleared most of the weed, it is necessary to provide food for it over a longish period so that the tench expect to find it there all the time. This is done by baiting the swim regularly until the fishing is to start.

There are countless ways of doing this and I would hesitate to say which was the best. Ordinary mashed bread, tightened with a little bran and with the addition of a few chopped worms is perhaps as good a medium as any, but there are many to choose from. One of the most successful tench days my brothers experienced was when they baited a swim several times with manure containing brandlings. I was unable to be with them on opening day but I assisted in the preparations. The swim was thoroughly dragged, baited with the manure, and then dragged again to spread the food around and to bury it in the mud. Our theory was that the tench would spend much longer in the swim if they had to work for their keep and the fact that the brandlings were well distributed kept them active all the time. On opening day over fifty tench were taken, the majority of them being over 4 pounds, with a few 5 pounders thrown in for luck.

Similar results have been achieved by using the flesh of swan mussels and applying the same procedure so that the tench did not find their food too easily. Any weed which the drag has missed is invariably uprooted by the tench as they grub around for the food in the swim, and this also is a big help.

Another method, but one which almost invariably attracts small fish as well, is to tie a bag of meat offal to a stake set in the middle of the swim. In time the meat becomes 'blown', and maggots form and drop into the swim to the fish below. Where large numbers of small rudd are present, however, it is not advisable to use this method. It is true that accumulations of small fish often attract the tench to the area, but they can be a nuisance when fishing starts. Oxblood used in conjunction with ordinary bread and bran groundbait is another great attractor. After a few hours in the container it congeals and forms a jelly-like substance and it is in this state that it is at its best. I feel that its close association with bloodworms (the larvae of chironomid flies which are so attractive to tench) is probably the reason.

Whatever method of pre-baiting is used, however, it is essential that it be done regularly at least three times a week. The oxblood should not be used until the night before the fishing begins, and on that night the groundbaiting should be lavish, and if possible continued at intervals through the night.

Many people have written to me from time to time asking about oxblood. They seem to be of the opinion that it is a secret and infallible bait, but I assure them that they are wrong. There is nothing new and nothing secret about oxblood groundbait. It was used in my father's day and I have no doubt it was used in his father's day too. There is no secret about acquiring it, you merely take a bucket to the nearest slaughterhouse on the days the beasts are being killed. For a few shillings you can acquire sufficient for a weekend's fishing, but do not run away with the idea that, here at last, is the answer to all tench-fishing problems. Blood will attract eels; it will attract pike and it will also attract tench, but it does not necessarily follow that the attracted tench will take any hookbait you care to offer them. It's not always as simple as that.

The idea of pre-baiting and swim preparation, however, is to get tench into the swim ready for catching and this means that they must be attracted from distant parts and accumulated in the swim. Spreading the groundbait over a wide area helps in this respect but it is also a good idea to drag channels in the surrounding weed leading to the cleared pitch. These channels should be cut in a 'round the clock' fashion and the longer they are the better. The channels as well as the swim should be baited for the first week or so and it will be found that many tench explore them, feeding en route, until they come to the swim proper. In this way tench can be drawn into the area from a long way away.

If pre-baiting programmes are out of the question because of distance or club rulings, etc., I think it is advisable to leave the preparations until the night before the fishing. The swim should then be cleared thoroughly of all weed and heavily baited ready for the following morning. Do not worry about the disturbance frightening the tench; they are most inquisitive creatures and I have never known the drag to keep them away for long. By morning the mud will have settled and the tench will, in all probability, be active in the swim. In gravel-bottomed waters such as small pits there is perhaps no necessity for such drastic measures. Often weed clearance is unnecessary and only a light pre-baiting is required. In these circumstances I think it is best to use ordinary samples of the intended hookbait. A couple of dozen balls of paste, a few pinches of flake or a handful of lobworms introduced daily if possible will 'educate' the tench into expecting them.

Generally speaking, the bigger the water the heavier the pre-baiting should be, but a lot depends on the numbers of tench present in the water. Waters such as the lakes at Wotton Underwood and Woodstock hold thousands of big tench, and it would be almost impossible to overfeed them. Smaller and less populated waters would respond to a less extravagant programme.

**Tactics and hookbaits**

The numbers of baits which have successfully accounted for tench are legion and it would be impossible to say which was the best. I believe that there is no such thing as a 'best' bait and when I fish for tench I like to take an assortment if possible.

Lobworms and bread are, however, the most popular with anglers, and generally speaking, one or other of these baits will suffice. They may be fished either on a leger, float, or leadless tackle and if the tench are 'on' there is no mistaking the bites when they come.

'Big baits for big fish' is probably the soundest approach, and where large numbers of tench are present, it is only necessary to fish with a large bait on the bottom. Irrespective of the tackle employed, the bites will be slow and decisive and there is no need for quick striking.

There are times, however, when the tench show no interest in large baits and prefer very small ones instead. Having watched many tench feeding from my boat on Wotton Lakes, I am convinced that baits are inside tench's mouths a lot more often than is generally supposed. While tench are sometimes averse to taking a big bait, they will often suck in and blow out a small one several times before either accepting or rejecting it. In many cases the bait is not taken because the tench are not feeding in the true sense of the word. They appear to be obeying a reflex which causes them to suck in and blow out each piece of food they encounter. Nevertheless it must be agreed that, if the bait finds its way into a tench's mouth, it constitutes a bite which should be struck at. Obviously a leger or a leadless tackle would not register these bites and something much more sensitive is necessary. The bait must lie on the bottom but the tackle has to be arranged so that these very quick bites are indicated. The generally accepted style of fishing

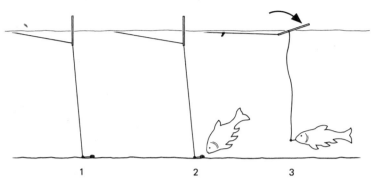

*Figure 14*    The 'lift' method in action

in these circumstances is nowadays referred to as the 'lift method' (*Figure 14*).

The tackle consists of a small peacock quill attached to the line at the bottom end only, by means of a plastic or rubber band. The hook is tied direct to the reel line and one large shot is pinched on about 2 inches above it. The tackle is set slightly deeper than the water being fished and all is drawn taut until the float cocks. Some adjustment is necessary until the correct depth is found and the tackle should be scaled up or down according to the manner in which the tench are biting. I have known times when it has been necessary to use a mere two inches of quill and a B B shot stopped no more than an inch from the hook.

At this stage I should point out that it is essential to put the rod in rests and wait for the bites to come. Any attempt to hold the rod merely causes the float to keel over and the whole set up is spoiled. The hand may, of course, rest lightly on the rod if desired but, despite the quickness of the bites, I have never found this necessary.

The bite is invariably indicated by the float lifting up and lying flat on the surface of the water. The strike should be made when the float is still rising.

The 'Lift Method' is probably the best all-round style of fishing for tench in near-bank swims. It is easily adaptable to any size of hook, bait or line strength. The distance between hook and shot may be varied from 2 feet to 2 inches in a matter of seconds and the rig will deal with slow and decisive bites as well as the 'finicky' type of bite I have just explained. All types of bait from maggots to large lobworms may be used on this outfit and if a float is at any time deemed unnecessary it is a simple matter to remove it without untying the hook. The small float ring which is left on the tackle does no harm and is readily available if the float is required again.

Where long-range fishing is necessary the leger will have to be used and, while it is not as sensitive as the 'lift method' it will be found that the bites are usually decisive when they come. The pick up of the fixed-spool reel should be left in the 'off' position so that the line may run out unhindered. A piece of silver paper folded on the line or a small twig resting lightly on the line above the reel will help to keep all taut but will allow the line to run freely when the bait is taken.

If the tench are taking boldly there seems to be no need for either floats or leads and if the tackle is comprised merely of a line, hook and bait, the bites will be even more decisive. Baits of course must be on the heavy side for this type of fishing. Lobworms, paste or flake are suitable; crust cubes must have extra weight to take them to the bottom.

One of the main problems encountered on many tench waters is the avoidance of the hordes of small fish which are invariably present. There are few tench lakes which do not breed an abundance of small roach, rudd or perch and these hungry infants make short work of baits intended for a more worthy species. It is essential to groundbait fairly heavily in order to attract the tench, but the very act of doing so also attracts many hundreds of small fish into the area. This can be frustrating at times. Rudd and roach often appear to remain active even after dark and there seems to be no ideal time of day or night when they may successfully be avoided.

The accepted method of avoiding the smaller and unwanted species is the use of outsize baits and it is true to say that this method often meets with a fair degree of success. On the other hand small bream and roach will make short work of even the largest piece of paste if it is left long enough for them to work on.

There are times, however, as I have already mentioned, when the tench themselves are not interested in outsize baits and have to be sought with smaller baits and this makes the problem even more difficult. Very often, during the latter part of the season, tench feed in a preoccupied manner upon very small organisms which lie beneath the surface of the mud. Such is the urgency of their feeding that they are apparently unable to recognize the existence of other and larger types of food. This type of feeding is often indicated by the large sheets of minute bubbles which rise to the surface of the water from time to time as the tench disturb the mud below. This action causes the release of many minute forms of life which are intercepted by the roach and rudd lying in wait a foot or more off the lake floor. It will be seen, therefore, that the presentation of a small bait is made extremely difficult and more often than not it is devoured by the small fish before it has time to reach the bottom.

One way of overcoming this is to enclose the bait in a ball of soft mud which will take it down to the bottom quickly and avoid the small fish en route. The fact that it is hidden from the tench is comparatively unimportant because they are actually engaged in the process of digging into the mud for food which is concealed therein.

It would be wrong to assume that this is the complete answer to the problem, however, for there is no guarantee that the bait will be taken even if it is located. There are times when the tench are interested in only one type of small organism which is very readily obtainable at that time. The attitude is similar to that of a trout feeding upon one particular type of surface fly. Very difficult for the angler to assess and even more difficult to imitate. As far as the tench angler is concerned, imitation is impossible and even if the type of food is correctly assessed it is often impossible to present it on a hook. The only possible solution to the problem is to wean the tench on to other food and this can be somewhat difficult. The food must be composed of a great number of identical particles and must be introduced in fairly large quantities to compete with the natural food. It must also sink quickly enough to avoid the small fish waiting at mid-water. One bait which answers all these requirements is stewed wheat. It is clean and wholesome, not unpleasant to handle, and being heavy, it sinks quickly. Once on the bottom it settles into the soft mud and, with any luck at all, will be discovered by the industrious tench as they dig. If sufficient quantities are introduced over a fairly wide area there is an even chance that the tench will accept the individual grains as natural items of food (see also remarks on particle baits, pages 25–31).

Experience has proved that it is essential to fish with only one grain of wheat on the hook and any attempt to cover a large hook with several kernels is unlikely to succeed. This means, of course, that comparatively small hooks have to be used but a No. 12 or 10 round bend tied direct to a 4 or 5 pound reel line is a very substantial rig. A lift tackle with a slightly heavier shot than usual should be employed. The extra weight of the shot will ensure that the hookbait is in the mud

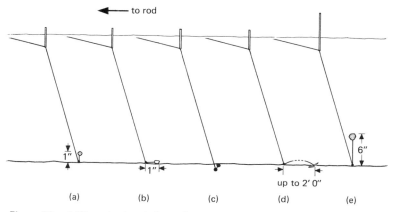

*Figure 15* 'Lift' method variations: A position of bait when using crust; B paste or flake; C wheat (larger shot); D lobworms; E crust for rudd in rough conditions (long float)

along with the other grains (*Figure 15c*). Bites are again indicated by a slow lift of the float and a rod with a fairly quick striking action is necessary to deal with them.

All tench do not behave thus, however, and in many cases it is only necessary to use a bait which the small fish cannot tackle. Among the best of these is the freshwater mussel which is found in most tench waters. The whole of the flesh may be used as hookbait and, while the small fish may attack it, the decisive, run-away bite will not come until a large tench picks it up confidently. I should perhaps make it quite clear that tench usually require 'educating' into taking mussel baits and that substantial groundbaiting with mussel flesh is usually necessary before they will succeed as hookbaits. There are many ways of fishing mussel baits and my preference, when possible, is to use the floatless, leadless tackle baited with a whole mussel and to wait for a decisive run-off. The tweaks and pulls of the small fish are not so noticeable, nor so disconcerting, as when a float tackle is used. One can at least be certain that the bait has not been eaten by small fish no matter how long it has been out.

When small baits are indicated the mussels can be cut into portions and very small snippets used on float tackle.

It is generally accepted that tench fishing should begin at first light, and tradition has it that morning mists and still, oily looking waters are a tench angler's dream come true. Undoubtedly there is a great pleasure to be derived from these conditions, and as long as the sun remains off the water, sport is likely to be good. Clear nights and early morning mists, however, often mean that the sun, when it rises, will be a blazing ball of fire all day long until it drops below the horizon at evening time.

This type of weather is all right for the angler who is just 'getting away from it all' but it is not much good to the man who wants to catch tench. The short time before the sun rises is often very profitable in a well-baited tench swim, but as the day gets older, sport gets slower until it finally ceases altogether. I have known times when orthodox tench fishing has been a waste of time after six a.m. and I am not so keen on traditional tench mornings. I do not want my fishing confined to a couple of hours in the morning and I prefer dull, windy or even squally conditions if I intend to fish all day. I like early-morning fishing of course but it isn't everyone who likes to rise at three a.m. to be fishing by dawn; in many cases public transport makes it impossible. This leaves one with the day-time fishing and considerably reduces one's chances – but it does not mean that tench cannot be caught in the day time.

Tench seldom feed well in strong sunlight, but a little observation and thought will often offer the right answers to this particular tench-fishing problem.

One of the main considerations is the depth of swim. I have found that water over nine or ten feet deep is more likely to produce tench during the day than the shallower water. But of course these deeper swims seldom produce fish before eight a.m.

Choice of swim, therefore, is very important, and depends entirely upon what you expect to get out of it.

Do you want a couple of hours fast fishing followed perhaps by twelve hours when the swim is completely dead? If so, choose the shallower 4 to 5 foot deep swim and groundbait it liberally, before fishing it at crack of dawn.

Or do you want to pick up the odd tench every now and then all through the day, even though the early morning fishing produces little or nothing? If so, choose a swim 9 or 10 feet deep and stick to it all day. (I am of course still referring to the average depth tench lake and not deep-flooded gravel or clay pits which need a different approach.)

In either case I would hazard that the numbers of tench caught over a period would be about equal.

Shallow swims can be 'encouraged' to fish on for a little longer by using the drag. I have found that very often a good raking will bring the tench back on feed for a while but extra groundbait does not interest them at all.

I have watched tench slowly leave a swim as the sun rose higher, leaving a white carpet of groundbait on the bottom. I have watched the trails of bubbles herald their return after a raking session.

It doesn't always work and when it does it is only a temporary measure, but it is well worth trying. It is said that the tench are curious creatures and that curiosity brings them back into the swim, but I think that the lessening of the light caused by the raking is also to some extent responsible.

While some tench get into the soft weed as the sun rises, some others retire into the marginal rushes and continue to feed.

The amount of disturbance caused by their searchings makes their whereabouts obvious and though they are not the easiest of fish to catch, they can be caught on small baits. The bait should be fished as near to the stems as possible, preferably on a floatless, leadless tackle and should be allowed to sink under its own weight (*Figure 16*).

If it is taken it will be taken quite decisively before it reaches the bottom.

A long rod with a stiffish butt action is an advantage with this type of fishing as it is often necessary to *push* the fish out of trouble.

Towards evening some of the tench will begin to feed again in the baited swims, but in some waters a very different type of feeding commences in the margins, especially where there has been a build-up

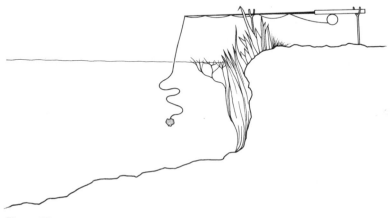

*Figure 16*

of warm water. I refer to surface feeding and, in one pond in particular, I catch quite a lot of tench on floating crusts.

At first the tench appear to be rolling and basking, but a few loose crusts quickly start the rudd feeding and these, in turn, cause the tench to take interest.

I have caught them thus in less than a foot of water and this is one case of tench and rudd feeding together in the margins. As a rule they seldom mix and if rudd are present in the margins I find that the slowly sinking bait method does not catch the tench – simply because they are not there.

Often the tench will take floating crusts well into the night but I prefer to fish for them then on the bottom in the orthodox style, and I shall deal with this later.

Slowly sinking baits often account for tench in open swims and my experience has shown that this often happens when the weather is hot but overcast. I offer no explanation as to why it should be, because I do not know why a confirmed bottom feeder should suddenly begin to take food which is not on the bottom. Many times, when weather conditions have been heavy and warm, my bait has remained untouched for long periods but has been taken immediately I have rebaited and cast again. This caused me to sit up and take notice and over a period I found that the tench were, in fact, taking the bait before it reached the bottom. When such conditions prevail nowadays I find it best to remove the shot completely and to fish with a self-cocking float. It is a fishing which is far removed from orthodox tench-fishing because the bait is being continually cast, allowed to sink and then retrieved. The results are usually better when the bait sinks on the very edge of the soft weed beds but the whole area should be searched when fishing in this manner. I have never known small baits to be necessary for this type of fishing and my main successes have been when the bait used was an outsize lobworm. At times I have fished with a large lobworm suspended from a float less than 2 feet below the surface, and I have taken many tench in this manner. This style of fishing must not be confused with the marginal fishing I have just explained. Here I am concerned with swims which are far removed from the margins and which are surrounded by soft weed and not rooted plants such as reeds and rushes. It has been suggested that previous disturbance of the mud by feeding tench has released a certain amount of food which is now suspended in the water and that the tench have moved up from the bottom to locate it. It has also been

F. J. T. relaxed but ready

suggested that the tench have moved up from the bottom to enjoy the warmer water near the surface. Either suggestion could be true, but there seems to be no concrete answer. The food which the tench have released from the mud would surely be very tiny and it is doubtful if they would then take an outsize lobworm. I have usually found, too, that if tench seek the warmer upper layer of water, they do so to rest and not to feed. However, whatever the explanation it is well worth remembering that tench can be taken at all depths in certain conditions.

Until now I have assumed that the tench angler wishes to catch tench only, and I have explained methods whereby the smaller and unwanted species may be avoided.

There are certain waters, however, where the only really certain way to succeed in catching tench is to catch a lot of small fish too. There are several lakes of my acquaintance where the methods used to avoid small fish only result in the bait remaining unnoticed by the tench too. In these waters I find that it is better to go all out to catch the small fish and wait for the odd tench to put in an appearance. One might almost say that the tactics to employ are those of the match man. Small hooks and baits are necessary and the swim should be fed continually with feed which attracts the small fish. It means that large numbers of small fish will have to be caught before the tench come along, but there is a certain amount of excitement involved. Obviously the ideal baits to use are maggots and they must be fished on a sensitive outfit so that all bites are registered. The swim should be fed sparingly but *very frequently* to keep the small fish active until the tench arrive. Sooner or later will come a bite which, although not noticeably different from the others, results in the hooking of something vastly different from what has been caught previously. This is the exciting time, for the tackle being used is not meant to deal with fighting tench. As a rule, however, there can be no compromise with regard to tackle and any attempt to scale it up will affect the results. I have found this method to be extremely suited to canals in which the tench are spread over a wide area. No one expects to catch a lot of tench in these waters but two or three in a mixed bag is a satisfactory achievement.

Although tench-fishing is usually considered to be a stationary type of fishing whereby the tench are attracted to a given area, it is often possible like Mahommed and his Mountain, to go to the tench instead. There are many areas of very shallow water in most tench lakes, and stalking tench in these shallows can be a very interesting type of fishing. A tin of worms and a loaf of bread are all that are required in the way of bait. A good casting rod, a line of about 5 pounds breaking strain and a No. 6 hook complete the equipment. The tench may be located in several ways, but generally speaking they are betrayed by mud clouds or surface bubbles as they feed. These tench are happy wanderers as a rule and their path may be ascertained by the general direction of the bubbles or mud clouds. Sometimes they can be seen ploughing their way through the silk weed, sometimes a bulge in the soft weed is the only indication of their presence. Generally speaking, however, as long as they are active they can be caught.

Some degree of stealth is necessary but nothing like that required when stalking carp in the same manner. Tench are not so easily scared as carp and a few bad casts need not have too bad an effect on the fishing. There is no point in standing up in full view of the fish, however, and advantage should be taken of available cover. Having ascertained the path which the tench appears to be taking (these fish have to be dealt with individually as a rule) it only remains to put a bait out where it is likely to be intercepted. Many times the tench will change direction at the last moment and another cast is then necessary if it is to be caught, but this is half the fun. Where a tench is seen to have its head down in earnest, an accurate cast into the middle of the bubbles or mud cloud is often all that is necessary. Do not expect a run-away type of bite, however, for these tench are feeding methodically and eating their food before moving on. A few twitches of the line are all that can be reasonably expected and the strike should not be delayed too long. Here and there a few worms or pieces of flake may be distributed in the path of the tench to allay suspicion, but this is not entirely necessary.

A hooked tench in these conditions behaves somewhat differently from a tench hooked in deeper water. It does not bore – it bolts, often at an amazing speed! This means, of course, that a very firm pressure has to be applied to stop it from burying itself in the soft weed. I have suggested a line of 6 pounds breaking strain and a No. 6 hook, but it may be necessary to increase both the line strength and the hook size in very weedy conditions.

Most of the baits I have mentioned so far have been fairly orthodox and, generally speaking, a supply of all the baits mentioned should prove adequate for any day's tench fishing. Nevertheless, there are times when a complete change from the orthodox will bring results. It has already been shown that unorthodox tactics often succeed; so, too, will unorthodox baits.

Very often, during the late summer, recognized tench swims often fail to produce fish despite the fact that there is every indication that they are present and active. Heavy groundbaiting probably tends to make the swim 'stale', and everyday baits such as paste, flake, worms and even freshwater mussels are not accepted as readily as they were during the early part of the season. At such times a certain amount of experiment with hookbaits can turn a blank day into a notable one.

My brothers and I have caught tench on an amazing number of 'silly' baits, ranging from pieces of tomato to black slugs, and always on days when they were apparently 'off'.

One of our favourite baits in these circumstances is puffed wheat breakfast cereal. It is an extremely difficult bait to use and cannot be relied upon to remain on the hook for more than a couple of minutes. As it is extremely buoyant it cannot be used as groundbait, and in order to keep it close on to the bottom the shot must be placed very near to the hook. It fishes better if it is allowed to rise about an inch from the lake bottom. After a few minutes immersion it will soften and very often float off the hook and come popping up to the surface, which means that continuous re-baiting is necessary. The bites are hardly detectable and the slightest movement of the float must be struck at. It is *not* a bait for the angler who likes to sit and watch for a good bite, for there is no such thing when fishing with puffed wheat. To me it is a far more difficult bait to use than hempseed, but it has accounted for many tench when all other baits have failed. Other unorthodox baits which come to mind, all of which have taken tench at one time or another, are snails, bacon rind, cake, honey paste, raw meat, hempseed paste, fat ham, bloodworms, caddis grubs, wasp grubs, hard-boiled egg, sausage, rusk paste, cheese and a paste into which oxblood has been moulded. All of these baits succeeded on days when the tench were apparently off feed, but there is no way of proving that they were taken in preference to the more orthodox baits. It is possible that the tench would have taken an ordinary bait anyway if we had waited a little longer.

In my experience, however, I have found that it pays to change baits frequently when the tench are not in real feeding mood. Just as the salmon angler or the pike fisherman changes his lure, so should we change baits frequently when things are not going well.

It pays to stray from the orthodox methods and orthodox baits from time to time. Tench-fishing has followed traditional lines too long and we are still basing our methods on the advice handed down to us from our grandfathers. There have been many instances in the past of days when tench were fairly hurling themselves on to baited hooks, and it is from such days as these that traditional tench-fishing methods have sprung. The advice our grandfathers handed down to us was not wrong; it was incomplete, and until we learn to remove ourselves from traditional and old-fashioned methods, many of the large tench in this country will remain uncaught.

My advice in this respect is to refuse to accept the 'rules' of tench-fishing and set out to prove them wrong! Try the unorthodox when all else fails, and remember that it is on the days when you have fished for hour after biteless hour that the very largest tench may be caught. Reference to the records reveals that the near-record specimens have very seldom formed part of a big catch.

### Boat fishing

Many thousands of tench are caught from boats every season, and there are many waters where few tench could be caught at all were it not for the fact that boats are available. In the majority of cases these boats are merely flat-bottomed punts which are rowed into position and held by a fore and aft anchor. Quite honestly if my tench-fishing had to be limited to fishing from an anchored punt I would give up tench-fishing. I can think of nothing worse than trying to fish the 'lift method' from a boat which is held only by anchors and which contains another occupant besides myself. I will go so far as to say that it is impossible to fish in the delicate manner which the 'lift method' demands from an unstable platform. The whole essence of 'lift-method' fishing lies in keeping the line taut from float to rod tip and the lightest movement by any member of the 'crew' upsets the whole set up and causes the float to keel over. False bites are being registered every few minutes because someone reaches for the bait or winds in to re-cast. Heavier and less sensitive float tackle does not behave properly when there is movement in the boat and even legering becomes almost impossible. Single-handed it is possible to fish reasonably well because the only movement of the boat is caused by oneself and the false movements of the float or bite indicator are recognizable. But who wants to sit in a boat in the middle of the lake on his own? I don't because, to me, half the enjoyment in fishing is derived from the company of my friends. This does not mean that tench can't be caught from an anchored punt, however, it merely means that, for me, much of the enjoyment is taken out of fishing because I am unable to fish as I would like to.

This may sound strange coming from someone who is well known to have fished for countless hours from a boat, and I should make it quite clear that my objection is not to the boat but to the method of making it stationary. I share a very large converted pontoon on which my friends and I sleep, eat and fish for long periods. It is dry inside and a folding canopy allows us to fish in the worst of weather without getting wet. But we do not use anchors to hold it in position; we use stakes which are driven into the mud. Our boat then becomes a rigid platform and not a boat in the true sense of the word. It gets us from point A to point B with a certain amount of difficulty because of the large area which is out of the water, but once in position it is no more than a stable platform from which to fish. Our method is to use four long poles which are driven into the bottom of the lake at the four corners of the boat. These are placed as near to the sides of the boat as possible so that the boat is in fact wedged between them. These are then lashed securely with ropes to fixtures on the sides of the boat so that no movement is allowed. As an extra precaution the tops of the fore and aft poles, which are now some 8 or 9 feet out of the water, are bent towards each other so that they form two archways across the boat and are then securely lashed together. In this fashion all movement of the boat is minimized, and apart from an occasional tightening of the ropes should the poles sink deeper into the mud, there is no need for any further attention.

It will be seen from this, however, that there can be no disagreement regarding the choice of the swim to be fished. The business of fixing the boat is rather a lengthy one and there can be no question of moving to a new swim after the first hour or so. In view of this my brothers and I fish the same swim for several weeks before cleaning out a new one. The cleared area is marked with corks and the boat is staked on the edge of the weeds and not in the clear water. We feel that the presence of a small amount of weed between the boat and the fish offers a certain amount of cover.

Although the staking down of the boat takes a long time and has a few disadvantages in other respects, we feel that this is by far the best way of making a stable fishing platform and I cannot understand why the idea is not used more. The same method can quite easily be applied to an ordinary fishing punt, or any other type of vessel. I have even used it with a rubber dinghy on occasions. If instead of rusty chains and anchors, hire boats were supplied with four strong sapling poles I feel sure that much better fishing would be the result. In extremely deep water and of course in hard-bottomed lakes, there is no alternative to using the anchors. It is worth remembering, however, that a boat remains more stable when *all* the anchor chain is paid out. A lot of drift occurs when boats are anchored on a tight chain. A certain amount of experience is necessary before the boat can be manoeuvred to the correct spot and at the same time making sure that all the anchor chain is paid out. It can be done, however, and it is worth the extra time involved. Even so it is never as satisfactory as a boat which is securely staked.

Generally speaking, boat anglers pay particular attention to wind direction and usually try to anchor the boat so that the wind is blowing from behind. This provides a lee in the swim and makes fishing a lot more comfortable, but there are times when it will pay to consider factors other than the wind. To me, the most important consideration is the position of the sun. There is very little pleasure in fishing into the sun – it is in fact almost impossible to watch a float with the sun's reflection almost blinding one. I would rather fish into

June tench from a boat

the wind with the sun behind me! I can combat the wind, but I cannot blot out the sun! I have had a great deal of experience in fishing for tench from boats and I am aware of the many snags involved, but I have never known extreme stealth and caution to be necessary. I have been in the company of anglers who have angrily 'hushed' when I have dropped the landing net across the bows with a thud; I have also been with anglers who couldn't have made more noise if they'd tried. I have never known it make any difference to the tench at all. I well remember how I cringed and shuddered each time an elderly gentleman acquaintance knocked his pipe out on the side of the boat. The rattle could be heard across the lake, but it did not put the tench off feed. I do not suggest that every boat angler should go out of his way to make a noise while fishing; I do assure you, however, that you need not worry too much if you drop the bait tin!

One of the accepted problems of tench-fishing from a boat is that of a hooked fish diving underneath and wrapping the line round the pole or the anchor chain. The recognized way of dealing with it is to put the rod under water and bully the fish out. In all my years' experience of boat-fishing I have only known three fish to make for the underneath part of the boat and only one of them ever succeeded in making it! To me it is an almost non-existent problem and I find that very few fish move in the direction of whatever is holding them. Rather do they bolt off in the opposite direction and try to put as much space between it and them as they possibly can. When this first run is checked they bore doggedly towards the bottom, changing direction every few seconds, but are seldom uncontrollable.

Perhaps the reason for my seldom experiencing these attempts to reach the underside of the boat is the fact that I use a long rod. I find that I am able to cast, strike and play a fish much better with a long rod and should one approach the boat it is a simple matter to push it away. I have used short rods from boats on occasions, but I can never understand why they are almost invariably advocated. We see short 7 and 8 feet rods advertised as boat rods but I cannot see where the advantage lies. How can you float fish in 12 feet of water for instance, with a rod of 7 or 8 feet? And why not take the same rod you would use from the bank anyway? I would seldom use a rod less than 10 feet long when boat fishing for tench, and I am happier with a 12 footer. Tackle control is much easier with a long rod, and a fish can be steered away from the trouble spots much more easily.

I am a great believer in fixed-spool reels and agree whole-heartedly that in many branches of fishing they are essential. I still feel, however, that there is a certain amount of pleasure to be derived from playing a fish on a centre-pin reel and I love to use one on a boat. This is purely personal preference, and I am not suggesting that centre-pins are better for boat-fishing. I do suggest, however, that fixed-spool reels are unnecessary when tench-fishing from a boat and that there is a lot of enjoyment in using a centre-pin.

It is the policy of many groups of angling friends to pool their baits and groundbaits in the interests of packing and travelling, but I think it is much wiser to travel self-contained when the fishing is to be done from a boat. There is nothing more annoying than to have to pass the worm tin at the precise moment when your float is beginning to perform some interesting gyrations and all your concentration is needed.

### Tench at night

A lot has been written about carp-fishing after hours of darkness, and nowadays, when one talks of night fishing, carp automatically spring to mind. Carp, of course, are largely nocturnal in habit but they can also be caught in the day time by a variety of methods. It is strange, therefore, that so little has been written about tench-fishing after dark, for, although tench are reputedly early morning and evening feeders, they can be caught at all hours of the day and night. It is now standard practice to pursue carp during the night, and it can be very exciting or very boring according to one's temperament. I find it hard to understand why anglers who are prepared to sit awake all night for one carp will not give tench the same treatment.

Long spells of hot weather and low water, blazing sun and cloudless skies are not the best conditions for tench-fishing and the brief spells before sunrise on such mornings do not give an angler time to settle down to serious fishing. It can be grand fun, however, to arrive at the water after the sun has set and to fish for tench until the sun's first rays hit the water.

It is an enjoyable fishing and one which does not have to be taken quite so seriously as carp-fishing. With carp one is almost afraid to breathe lest the slightest tremor puts the carp off for the rest of the night. No lights must be shown and even the match which lights one's cigarette must be shielded. Complicated rigs and bite alarms are often necessary and the line must be allowed to run freely off the spool immediately a carp takes.

With tench it is different. No bite alarms are really necessary, although there is no objection to one being used. It cannot spoil your chances but you do not *have* to use one. An ordinary centre-pin reel may be used and if no bite indicator is available the check can be set and the clicks, as it unwinds, will be indication enough that a tench has taken. Stamping about the banks, of course, will not help matters with any type of fishing but the occasional lighting up of a cigarette or spirit stove will not put tench off, and it can mean the difference between a comfortable night's fishing and an uncomfortable one. A cup of tea or a bowl of soup is very welcome after midnight on a cold night.

We've all fished for tench at one time or another from dawn till dusk without so much as a tremble of the float to indicate that tench are about. Those familiar sheets of bubbles which denote feeding tench have been absent and we've all wondered where the tench have gone. At times like these it is probable that they would have fed during the night if we had stayed on and fished in the dark. Nowadays I find it is more profitable to reverse the usual procedure of arriving early and leaving late, and to enjoy the best of both worlds by arriving late and leaving next morning.

Tench-fishing at night is very little different from fishing during the day. The baits are the same: lobworms, flake or paste. The same swims will fish at night as well as in the morning and evening, and orthodox groundbaiting procedure is satisfactory.

A floatless, leadless tackle is required, and here there is some difference between night and day-time fishing. Baits of bread or paste can be considerably larger than those used in the day time, and because of this the bites will be bold and decisive. A tench that tweaks at a small bait in the day time will run off with a large one at night and will soon be in weed if not stopped quickly. They can be stopped quite easily, however, because there is no need for ultra-fine tackle in the dark. A strong line can be used and put to good effect when a fish has to be stopped.

Where eels are present, worms are not a very good proposition and, unless one is fishing exclusively for eels, they can be an absolute menace. They have been known to take bread baits too, but as a rule a knob of paste or a cube of crust does not attract them.

Mussels, too, are another fine bait for tench in the dark. Where there are tench there are usually plenty of mussels to be found. Wade into the shallows, and grope around the rush stems and you will usually find sufficient for a night's fishing within half an hour or so. Chop some of them up and put them in with the groundbait. Use a whole mussel on a large hook for bait and wait for a decisive run off before striking. Some people find difficulty in opening mussels, but it is a simple procedure. The secret is to use a sharp knife and to insert it in between the shells at both sides of the 'hinge'. This allows the shell to open and the whole of the inside can be scraped out with the knife.

It has been written and generally accepted that carp move in certain mysterious ways at night and as a result many people who fish for tench at night believe that the tench behave likewise. This is not altogether correct, and while there are plenty of tench which move a long way during the dark hours there are many which do not move at all from their day-time haunts. Unlike carp, which almost invariably move out of the shallows on cold clear nights, tench often stay put. My brothers and I have caught large numbers of biggish tench in less than 2 feet of water at night, and I well remember Dick Walker catching a $5\frac{1}{2}$ pounder in water about 10 inches deep.

Margin-feeding tench are very determined creatures and I have known them push their way through water so shallow that their backs have been exposed. The attraction, on hard-fished waters, is obviously the bread which day-time anglers have discarded and I have known tench to take pieces of bread which have been literally half in the water and half on the bank!

Where such fish are encountered it is probably best to use surface crust baits. Some very large tench have been taken in this manner.

Very often, when the night is cold and clear, the tench in the shallows begin their feeding early but go off soon after midnight. This could mean that they have moved into deeper water or it could mean that they have finished feeding, but it often pays to introduce some more groundbait at this time. My brothers and I usually groundbait at eight p.m. and again around midnight, but a lot depends upon the numbers of fish in the swim. Generally speaking night fishing for tench is unnecessary as they can usually be caught well enough in the day time. Night fishing is merely a very pleasant addition to the day-time activities and one doesn't *have* to stay all night. Quite often, the first two hours of darkness are very exciting and these are then followed by several hours of inactivity. In many cases it would be advisable not to continue fishing after the first two hours but one never knows, with tench, just when they will start to feed again.

Night fishing of any kind can be boring or exciting depending on the mood of the fish, but it will *always* be tiring. Don't try to fish both day *and* night or you will reach a stage when you are no longer enjoying it. Find a shady tree and get you head down during the day – you'll fish all the better for it!

# 9 Eels

Eels are regarded by the majority of anglers as the bane of the fisherman's life. The very mention of the word 'eels' brings to their mind a slimy and wriggling creature which takes a bait intended for roach, perch or carp and proceeds to ball up their tackle into an impossible tangle. It is hopeless to try to 'play them out', they say, because there is no 'playing' an eel.

These words may be very true, and I have many times cursed the small eel which takes an outsize piece of paste or large lobworm intended for some other species of fish, but catching eels intentionally can be fun.

Most anglers know how to thread a dead fish on to the line as an eel bait, and how to wait for the eel to complete its first run after it has taken the bait, before striking. In my opinion this kind of angling is quite exciting and one which does not have to be taken too seriously. After a long spell in search of elusive carp or tench, a day (or a night) fishing for eels provides quite an entertaining 'time-off' period.

There is a great thrill in watching the line strip off the spool when a big eel takes and there is a great thrill in the two fights which follow – one in the water and one on the bank!

Maurice Ingham divides eels into two distinct classes, 'worm-eels' and 'fish-eels'. (The classification is obvious depending on the bait used). A 'fish-eel', however, should weigh at least 3 pounds, and while it is possible to catch eels of 3 pounds on worms, it is very rarely they are caught *under* 3 pounds on dead fish from the waters I fish. I am not at all sure that dead fish are the best bait for big eels, although the biggest eels I have landed have been caught in that way. The biggest ones I have hooked, though, have been when using worms either singly or in a bunch, and I have lost them either through breakage, or because the hook hold has given. That is the main trouble I find when using worms for eels. When do you strike? Do you wait for the eel to swallow the worms and chance the line being bitten through, or do you strike quickly and risk not hooking the eel properly? Big eels do not feed as often as smaller ones and having persuaded one to take the bait I like to be reasonably sure of my eel before striking. For this reason I rely on the dead-fish method as the chances of the line being bitten through are very much reduced. If the dead fish is stopped by a shot near the tail it cannot be blown up the line by the eel, and it remains in place making an effective 'gag' until the eel is landed.

I have tried using a short wire trace in conjunction with worm fishing, thinking that I could let the eel take as much time as it wanted without being able to bite through the line, but none of the bites I had developed into real eel runs. I have no doubt at all that the eels felt the wire and decided that all was not well, because in each instance the worms were rejected. Big eels are not stupid and they are very sensitive to resistance. During the day time they feed well out into the middle of the lake, but at night time they move in quite close to the banks.

If you are fishing for eels with dead fish as bait, feed the line off the reel as soon as you have a run. Make sure that the line goes directly into the water and does not get caught up in any bank herbage, because during this first run the eel is merely holding the bait in its mouth and will eject it at the first sign of resistance. Once it has decided to swallow the bait it *cannot* spit it out and if you pump and wind, pump and wind as hard as your tackle will allow, you will soon have it near the bank. What you do then will depend on the strength of your tackle. If it is strong, you can point the rod at it and slide it on to the bank. If not, I say without hesitation, use a net! A big carp net with a fine mesh is the best tool I have ever used to deal with big eels. Fancy gaffs have been advocated (and no doubt used) from time to time, but a big eel is a slippery customer and I prefer the net, provided it is a big deep one.

Having got the eel on the bank you must be prepared to deal drastically with it. Never mind about newspapers, or sacks or handfuls of sand. Fetch it one good clout on the back (directly above the vent is the best place) – stick a knife through its head, pinning it to the bank, and it will never move again.

I see no point whatsoever in returning eels to the water. They do quite a lot of damage to a fishery, devouring, as they do, vast quantities of spawn (particularly carp spawn) and small fish. All the eels I catch are eaten, either by myself and friends at the waterside or by friends at home who consider them a delicacy. I have no trouble in getting rid of eels – in fact, I have difficulty in getting enough to please all my friends. Many times a panful of eels has eked out the weekend's rations when I have been carp fishing off the beaten track.

Waters containing large carp usually contain large eels as well and it appears that what suits the one fish suits the other also. Both species thrive in the same water, and appear to feed under the same conditions with regard to water temperature. If the water temperature gets much below 57°F, it is doubtful whether you will catch many large eels, but they will feed on during the day when the sun is on the water and most other species have gone off feed completely. (This is not true of very deep still waters. Big eels are known to feed throughout the winter in many waters which are so deep that they are unlikely to become very warm even in summer.)

It has been said that eels will feed most ravenously either just before, during, or just after thunderstorms, but having fished under these conditions many times without a bite I do not pay too much attention to weather conditions. I am reluctant to fish for eels at night if there are carp to be caught, but I think night time is the best time of all to catch eels.

Eels in abundance

If you are contemplating a night's eel fishing it is as well to go prepared. Night fishing is a hazardous business at the best of times, but it can be worse than hopeless if you try to deal with big eels in the darkness unprepared.

Before you start, have ready seven or eight deadbait tackles made up with baits threaded on to a few inches of nylon (or wire) and attach a swivel at the end of each. Have also at hand a large sack, with a drawstring attached, hung up on a tree near by. A large tent, a torch, a knife and a stout stick are other items of necessity.

Prepare a groundbait of bread and bran, add some finely chopped fish and throw this out into the swim. Blood is a fine attractor of eels and this can be added to the groundbait as well if you like.

Stab your deadbait all over with a sharp knife before throwing it out – this ensures that the swim-bladder is punctured, allowing the bait to sink, and also acts as a further attractor. When you have a run, just follow the rules – wait till the run stops and starts again – get your fish on the bank and apply the 'pacifier'. Lower it into the sack – cut the line above the swivel and tie the sack up. Tie on a new bait and cast out again. These few preparations will save you endless bother with tangled lines and frayed tempers and you can get all your hooks and swivels back in daylight.

Fishing a private lake which contains among other fish some medium-sized eels, Peter Thomas and I noticed quite a lot of eels mid-water early one morning. Peter decided that one way to remove them would be to foul-hook them. Thus was born (to me anyway) the method known as 'eel snitching'. The 'snitch' is merely a large treble hook fixed *above* a small weight on an ordinary rod and line and it is used from a punt. The punt is paddled slowly across the lake, the 'snitcher' meanwhile standing on the bows looking for eels. Skill is needed to paddle the punt without scaring the eels and skill is needed to 'snitch' them, but the middle man, who merely does the unhooking, has to be a hero! I say it without blushing – I was the middle man. Fun? It was positively dangerous!

Peter Thomas has had a lot of 'snitching' experience as it is a method whereby he removes unwanted pike from his trout stream, and on this occasion he only missed three, but after the first few I began to wish that he was not so skilful!

His method was to lower the snitch over the eel's back until it hung below it – then a quick snatch and the eel was swinging in mid-air. Funny how it always seemed to swing in the direction of my ear!

The first one was hooked 'amid-ships' which was not so bad, but when they began to come aboard hooked in the tail I began to wonder who had the best job. Try holding a 2 pound eel by the head in a wet handkerchief, when its tail is thrashing a No. 2 treble in all directions and you'll see what I mean!

To help matters, those that had already been unhooked suddenly decided that sanctuary was to be found up my trouser leg and did their best to get there. In all we caught eight eels in about an hour, but if I go eel 'snitching' again I am going prepared – that is if I am expected to be middle man again.

I want a dozen prepared 'snitches', a knife, a sack and bicycle clips!

However, as I said before, whichever way you catch them, eels can be fun, but the fun really doesn't start until the eels leave the water.

Eel fishing, as far as I am concerned, is a light-hearted venture. I do not take it seriously and it simply serves to fill gaps between my more serious forms of fishing. There is no reason why it should not be taken seriously, however, and the eel record sets a target which will have to be pursued seriously if it is to be broken intentionally. The National Anquilla Club, formed in 1964, is made up of members who *are* seriously interested in eels. Their aim, I suspect, is the eel record and they are making special studies of freshwater eels with a view to developing new baits, tactics and techniques which are so obviously necessary for the enormous eels known to exist in, but never caught from, British waters.

There is scope for much serious angling with eels in mind and despite the fact that they are not readily caught, many waters contain eels about which little is known. During the 1963 freeze-up I found two record-sized eels from a water I had fished for many years. I had used worms, and occasionally, small fish baits there, but I did not until then know the eels existed. Wotton Lakes, in all my years of fishing, has produced only two eels. Another huge eel was lost when my brother Ken hooked it on light tackle. That fish could have been a 6 pounder according to those who witnessed it. Strangely enough, eels taken from the eel trap were part of the Wotton Estate's economy between the two world wars.

There are mysteries we shall never quite figure out. It is undoubtedly true that they can cross over land. It is true that they have an incredible sense of direction. It is true that they can detect smells or flavours in the water. Mark Sosin, an American biologist and author, states that the eel is capable of sensing a certain alcohol ($\beta$

phenyl-ethyl) in dilutions of less than a billionth of a drop in a large swimming pool!

I have long-lined for eels, speared them, trapped them in nets, and caught them with electro-fishing equipment, but though I have access to waters holding big eels, I can seldom work up enough enthusiasm to fish out a long session. Quite the largest eels I ever hooked were in an old salt mine complex in the Lancashire Fylde district. I landed them to over 3 pounds on totally inadequate tackle, but I hesitate to put a weight on those I lost. So many enormous eels have turned up in draglines and in dried-up canals that, despite the mystery which shrouds them, they must surely offer the record hunter a great chance of success.

# 10 Bream

When I first wrote this book I stated that I lived within a few miles of some of the best bream waters in the country. As I write, this is no longer true, but I see no reason to change my views on the Tring group of reservoirs. They were then, and still are, superb waters. Large bags of bream and very big individual specimens have been coming from Startops, Marsworth, Wilstone and Drayton for more years than I care to remember and, despite their great records, these waters have never become difficult to fish. Perhaps, because fishing is not allowed on Sundays, they have not been subjected to the same pressures as other day-ticket waters. They have their good and bad days like all other waters, but I have not found it necessary to fish with fine lines and tiny hooks. I have not regarded the choice of float or shotting pattern as important and, while I do not deny that sophisticated swim-feeders, fine links and tiny baits have succeeded well enough in the hands of experts in that field, I rate a simple leger tackle baited with bread, crust or paste, as being just as effective.

There have been times when big baits were well accepted and there have been times when almost any presentation proved unbelievably deadly. On days such as those, few and far between though they may be, bream with their heads down and feeding in earnest show no regard for tackle strength or bait size. Everything goes, and little skill is required to compile a big catch. In the main, however, relatively small baits have proved to be the best all round proposition over the years. By relatively small I mean, perhaps, a pinch of flake or a $\frac{1}{4}$ inch cube of crust on a size 10 hook. That presentation, by modern match-fishing standards, is still fairly crude. It could hardly be compared with – say – a single caster on a size 20 hook, which is a not unusual match angler's presentation. The bream at Tring, in my experience, respond to simple everyday fishing and I like it that way. Complicated tackles and delicately balanced rigs become essential at times in most waters, but there is no point in making things more difficult than they really are.

Tring bream are wanderers and it has always been difficult to attract and hold them in one spot. When that *has* been achieved the results have been incredible. Reports of fish and bags of fish from as far back as the 1930s until the present day have read like an angler's dream. I have had my share of good bream from Tring, but my catches have been very modest compared with those who devoted more time and effort, or who happened to be in the right place at the right time. I once put in a great deal of effort pre-baiting a swim at Wilstone and on opening day allowed several other anglers to fish it first. The swim responded well with fish up to $7\frac{3}{4}$ pounds and a few days later, when Ian Howcroft and I fished it at dawn we had a number of fish over 8 pounds. My own catch comprised five bream weighing $40\frac{1}{4}$ pounds. I took three fish over 8 pounds in as many casts and, although I have had many larger bags of fish, I have yet to take a better-quality catch. But that, compared with the bag compiled by Rod Lane and Ian Howcroft the following season in more or less the same spot, is now hardly worthy of mention. I forget the actual figures, but I know there were few fish under 8 pounds and that the largest were well into double figures. Both Rod and Ian had a $10\frac{1}{2}$ pounder each. All this took place between dawn and ten a.m. when

Ian Howcroft with a big Tring bream

both anglers tired of catching fish and adjourned to the Angler's Retreat to celebrate. Bream were still feeding when they left, but the swim yielded little after that. The following year, when Wilstone was opened to a night-fishing syndicate for the first time, John Howe took a tremendous catch of bream on opening day. His fish, some twelve in all, weighed up to about 12 pounds and were taken, oddly enough, *during the day* from Startops!

I have long believed that many bream tend to stay well out from the bank during the day time, and, having seen big shoals at Tring from time to time, *just* out of casting range, I tried to develop ways and means of getting to them with hookbait and groundbait.

It was my belief then, and experiences on some other waters help bear it out, that there *was always a chance* that the fish would begin to feed once the sun was off the water. I threw groundbait out with a throwing stick, used a catapult long before it became a matchman's maggot distributor, and generally tried to reach those distant fish by any means possible. I never quite succeeded in reaching the target area because the water remained high during the years I was making the attempt, but I did catch a lot of average bream and I learned much in the process.

Tring was my starting point as far as bream were concerned and future developments all stemmed from those early experiences. In the early days I was not a dedicated bream-fisher because I could never regard them as strong fighters but, in later years, I developed a greater respect for them and spent more time in their exclusive pursuit. The big bream from the Irish River Erne took up some of my holiday periods. I fished the Upper Thames in company with Peter Stone and Peter Drennan of Oxford, and I spent season after season fishing the whole weekend through for the elusive bream of a private Lincolnshire lake. I can claim success of a sort, but if that success had to be measured in terms of time and effort, the ratio would be low. How, therefore, am I able to discuss bream and bream-fishing in the confines of one short chapter when my experiences have been so wide and varied, yet spiced with only modest success?

Perhaps the simplest way would be to describe some of the methods used and known to be successful on a number of different waters. Baits and groundbaits differ little if any from those described in the tench chapter and if I had to come down in favour of one particular bait I would choose soft bread paste. A good bait for Tring bream was, and often still is, a moderate pinch of flake and two maggots.

English angler with a River Erne bream

Four Tring bream averaging almost 8 pounds each

Bream are expert whittlers and on those days when they are not taking boldly they will often remove the bread portion completely and finally take the remaining maggots. No one knows for certain that this is what happens, of course, but observation and experience suggest that this is the case.

Brandlings have proved to be excellent baits for summer, still-water bream and for autumn flood-water fishing in the River Thames. In a slack backwater, Peter Stone and I have occasionally caught bream in appalling conditions by using simple float tackle and brandling hookbaits. It has never been a very active style of fishing and bites have been few and far between, but by sitting it out and allowing the bait to drift around just off the bottom, we have caught bream when most anglers would have written conditions off as impossible. I take no credit for any bream I have caught in those conditions; Peter's observations and local knowledge were the key factors. It was he who set me off on the 'touch-leger' trail, though he will probably agree with me that in the early days we tended to watch the rod tip as well as feeling for the bites. When we began fishing rivers at night it was essential to be able to feel a biting fish. Peter would almost certainly outfish me on the Thames, but I think he would agree with me that touch-legering for bream is still not too well understood.

Today's swing and quiver tips have replaced, to some extent, the necessity to hold the rod and feel for the delicate bite of a river bream, but I have to admit that, while I do not decry their efficiency, swing and quiver tips do not let me *enjoy* my fishing quite as much as my *developed* touch-legering ability. I know anglers who state that they simply cannot relax while attempting to practise it and I think I know what they mean. It *is* important to be in a position to feel a sensitive bite and react to it without being tensed up and uncomfortable. You don't have to stare at a float or a swing tip or a quiver tip or a dough bobbin or anything else. You don't have to listen for a bite alarm to rattle or wait for a light to switch on, and although touch-legering demands that the rod be held, it still ought to be a very relaxed kind of fishing. I have been interested in the development of touch-leger rods in recent years, and my own particular choice of grip is with the line looped over the first finger of the hand holding the rod; in other words in the same position as it would be immediately prior to making a cast. I find the tip of my forefinger is very sensitive not only to pulls on the line but also to the slight relaxing of the line that indicates a slack-line bite. I find that a lightweight soft-actioned rod with a comparatively short handle is ideal. I can, if necessary, rest the front end of the rod on a rest while still keeping in 'finger touch' and the soft action of the rod helps me, personally, not to react violently to sharp bites. But I would not be dogmatic and say that this is the *correct* hold for touch-legering. I have friends who like to hold the line between the thumb and forefinger of the hand not holding the rod. I have others who like to use the same grip with the line running under the left hand and pulling gently against the little finger of that hand.

And I've no doubt there are anglers who have other ideas that are different again. I don't believe it matters as long as you're relaxed and comfortable, and able to concentrate on the *feel* of the tackle.

After a time the slow pulls of a good fish become distinguishable from the quick snatches of small roach and gudgeon. Sometimes only the slightest tremble can be felt, but some kind of sixth sense often tells me whether or not it is caused by a sizeable fish. That is something I cannot explain, but I am convinced that all anglers have had similar experiences.

I have only been involved in two bream catches exceeding 100 pounds. One was with Peter Stone in a Thames weir pool in the early 1960s, the other was with my brother Ken in a wide stretch higher up on the same river. On that occasion we fished all night for absolutely nothing and only began to catch fish when we were thinking of packing up next morning – proof enough that it often takes bream a long time to locate a groundbaited swim. On that particular morning our supply of groundbait had all been used up, but we managed to hold the shoal and weigh in 120 pounds of fish. Some were roach × bream hybrids; most were bream in the 2 to 4 pound category, but the best weighed 6 pounds. When Peter and I fished the weir pool we ran out of groundbait and bites stopped altogether until we were able to send for more. And that is one of the really strange aspects of Thames bream-fishing. Sometimes huge amounts of groundbait are needed while the fishing continues, but I recall one time when an overnight pre-baiting had accumulated bream in a far-bank swim, and when four excited anglers hooked fish on their first cast. We felt that the shoal had to be held if possible and introduced more groundbait at once. Bites ceased immediately and no more fish were caught that day. The moral, of course, is to wait until bites stop altogether before using more groundbait. While bites continue, leave well alone! A feeder link or similar kind of maggot distributor might be useful in these circumstances. Thames experts like Fred Towns and other members of the Oxford Specimen Group have already made great strides in this particular field. They tell me that it takes time and great patience, and that it is important to know how long each feeder takes to empty. So critical do they regard it that they have developed

Thames bream in the snow

feeders with different emptying rates to deal with a number of bream-fishing situations. They're still working at it as far as I know.

I have usually found early-season river bream difficult to locate; but I can think of one or two notable exceptions. I know several spots below weirs and overshots and in narrow bottlenecks where bream show up almost every June. The fact that they accumulate there early in the season suggests that they have chosen a livelier current area to recover from spawning, but there is no guarantee that they will remain. If anything the reverse is likely to be true because bream tend to move around a great deal in summer. They have big appetites and although big shoals gather together after spawning, they often split up into smaller groups and go their separate ways. Very often these large accumulations do not comprise a feeding shoal; it takes them some time to settle down to a feeding pattern. Nevertheless, it is always an advantage to know where the shoals are to be located and it is possible occasionally to employ feeder techniques to catch them. In fast currents, hookbaits and groundbaits seldom end up in the same place and modern feeders can be used to ensure greater accuracy.

Alternatively, a very stiff groundbait, made up with stale bread and one of the multi-meal groundbaits put in at the head of a fast-water swim will sink quickly and break up slowly. Barley meal is also a good drying agent for this kind of groundbaiting procedure. It 'milks' away very attractively.

And although it's a messy and inconvenient business, there's still a lot to be said for chopped worms/brandlings and ordinary soil. Lobs will work their own way into soil, clay or garden turf, if they're tipped into a bucket of it. Brandlings will have to be mixed in as they tend to bunch up. It takes time to get it all together, but it's a cheap form of groundbait and it will stay where it's put for the most part.

There have been reports of bream regurgitating smaller fish on being captured and Peter Stone has actually seen a Thames bream engulf a live bleak. This, plus the knowledge that many bream waters are grossly overstocked with small, minnow-sized fry, has prompted many anglers to ask if it would be advisable to fish for bream with either small live fish or artificial lures.

The truth is that most, if not all, species of fish eat smaller ones when the opportunity arises, and bream in a river are no different from goldfish in an ornamental pond in this respect. (Anyone who has tried to breed goldfish without arranging for some kind of protection for the

newly hatched fry, will not need any convincing from me that big
goldfish eat little ones!)

In Holland, where there are plenty of weed-free, slow-moving
waters, roach × bream hybrids are, reputedly, caught regularly on
superfine tackle and very tiny spoons.

We have never, to the best of my knowledge, sought seriously in
this country to catch coarse fish on lures, largely, I believe, because
very few of our waters are suitable. There are waters, however, where
these methods might well work if only they were allowed. I refer, of
course, to the big trout reservoirs. Sooner or later, coarse fish,
particularly bream and roach, begin to encroach into them all, and it is
by no means unusual for roach to take small lures, fry flies and other
'flies' dressed to represent small fish.

I have taken many coarse fish with weighted streamers and
bucktails; I have a friend who has taken a lot of dace by twitching a
sunken polystickle upstream on fly tackle. But I have only ever caught
one bream on a fly. That was a surface-fished mayfly intended for
rudd and I take no credit for its capture. My brother Ken, fishing a
well-known barbel hole in the Thames, hooked a huge fish some years
ago on a polystickle fly. Unfortunately we never saw the fish; it
escaped shortly after it was hooked, but he is quite convinced that it
was a barbel.

Since then he and I have spent a great deal of time fishing with
weighted streamer flies for all kinds of fish. We have enjoyed
experimenting and where it has been possible to *see* the fish, their
reactions have been remarkable. We have caught grayling and dace
on flies tied to look like minnows. We have caught big rudd from
under the rod tip and we have actually had reactions from carp. And,
of course, we've caught small zander.

Anglers have written to me from time to time telling of bream
caught on streamer flies and small spinners and I am in no doubt
whatsoever that, with perseverance, I could do the same; but I do not
believe it would be worth the tremendous effort involved. Nor do I
believe that lure fishing or live-baiting with small fish could ever
replace traditional bream-fishing methods.

In recent years developments have come about regarding luminous
floats and, thanks largely to Richard Walker, who pioneered the idea,
we are now able to float-fish in complete darkness. We no longer need
to illuminate the float in a torch beam. The torch-beam method
remains effective, however, and provided the light shines only *across*

and not *into* the water the fish are not scared. Float fishing for bream after dark helps to deal with the problem of missed bites peculiar to legering in many still waters. Using windbeater or driftbeater floats that show up well in a torch beam, I have reduced the number of missed bream bites by over 50 per cent; but I have never really been completely satisfied that I was doing the right thing. And I am always conscious of the fact that there may be other anglers present to whom my powerful torch beam could give offence.

Early attempts to make luminous floats with paint and strips of material that glowed in the dark after 'charging' in a torch beam, were unsuccessful but the *high-powered* beta light has brought about unbelievable improvements.

Beta-light float-fishing is a comparatively new and quite revolutionary kind of night-fishing. It would take a chapter to describe some of the problems and solutions involved and there are technical problems for which no satisfactory answer has been found so far. To understand why the low-powered beta lights used for butt indicators are not powerful enough for float-fishing, it is necessary to know that they are rated 190 M/L. The expensive commercial types sold loose for D I Y float making are rated 420 M/L (M/L = Micro Lamberts, I'm told, but it doesn't matter, the figure is the important part).

Malcolm Baldwin with a night's bream haul

These are visible at several rod lengths and because they have no heavy plastic coating they can be glued into suitable float stems. In the process about a third of their effective light is buried in the stem. Transparent plastic tubing can be used to house the unit so that it all remains visible, but extremely clear plastic tube that will allow *all* the light through is not easily obtained. Much of it may *look* clear but in fact it isn't quite as clear as it appears.

However, even with part of its power lost, a 420 M/L beta light shows up well. A lower-powered light has to be viewed from very close range and here's where the problem starts. You can sit close to it, fishing with your float only a few feet out, and see it perfectly. The trouble is that, from that angle, you can still see it when it has gone under, and you're never sure about bites unless they're so good that the float goes under a long way.

Looking at a more powerful beta-light float from a greater distance, however, means that the angle of sight is reduced and that the float disappears from view the second it goes under. Strange things happen with reflections in the water but bite registration is positive. If the float is shotted down so that only the beta light is clear of the water, the image is made to look twice as big. If it rides a little higher, two images appear. That doesn't matter as long as you're aware of what you're supposed to see.

As most night-fishing of this kind is likely to be practised in still water, there's a need for a float that offers little resistance to a taking fish and the obvious suggestion is a lift-type float with bottom buoyancy. Attaching a fairly heavy beta light to the slender antenna of such a float, however, tends to make it top heavy and difficult to balance. The top-heaviness can be counteracted by using a buoyant balsawood or polystyrene 'sight bob' on the tip and inserting the beta light into that.

Bites are then usually registered by a lift of the stem and as this happens the beta-light image splits in two and the two images separate completely before the float keels over and either lies flat on the surface or dives underwater. In the darkness the sudden appearance of two images looks weird, but when you realize that one is real and the other simply a reflection in the water, the whole thing becomes clear. Shotting these floats *has* to be sorted out in daylight. It's much too confusing to try and do it after dark.

High-powered beta lights are expensive, and although there are some cheaper ones available they are very much weaker and of no earthly use for float-fishing. They have other uses, however, and are good on swing or quiver tips.

Some kind of insurance against loss is therefore essential and if glue is used it should be well tested in water beforehand. I once thought I'd found the glue to end all glues. My beta light stayed put after hours of fishing (riding high on a float stem) but fell off when I left the tackle out in the rain. And here's an interesting point. It fell off during the day and I had to wait until night time before I could find it again.

The more I use beta-light-tipped floats the more intrigued with their possibilities I become. I haven't found all the answers yet, but my night-fishing for bream has been all the better for having used them.

I would suggest, however, that those who are anticipating using them should be extra careful about line strength. Make sure the reel line is sound and considerably stronger than the length below the float. That way you'll avoid expensive losses.

# 11 Roach

This chapter deals only with the kind of roach-fishing I think I understand: roaching in rivers of modest size and flow. Much of its content will apply to other waters, but in view of today's developments, I have to leave the specialist forms of roach-fishing practised in canals and still waters to those more qualified.

One of these days I may catch a really big roach and, if I do, it will be by sheer luck and nothing else. I say this, not because luck is essential to the catching of big roach but because I do not set out to catch them by design. There are many anglers who do, and who are much more qualified to describe the 'hows' and 'wheres' and 'whens' of big roach-fishing than I. To them a 2 pounder is a fish; one weighing 2 ounces under isn't! That's perhaps an exaggeration, and I hasten to add that no slight is intended, but it *is* an attitude of mind. There are roach and roach just as there are carp and carp, bream and bream, and so forth. One's attitude towards certain species can change over the years and it's not at all unusual for an angler to become engrossed – even fanatical – in the pursuit of fish that fall into a category above a certain standard. So we have men who set their sights on 2 pound roach and who are satisfied with nothing less. In my angling life I have only ever taken three over that weight. Two of those were accidental. I cannot think in terms of super specimens because I enjoy the simple pleasure of general roach-fishing too much. I do not want to catch small roach unless they are for use as pike baits, but there is something about the capture of a well-conditioned roach that defies description. I ask for no greater thrill than that of the sight of a deep-bodied $\frac{3}{4}$ pounder flashing and twisting in a lively current on a bright day. And if it happens to be one of a dozen or so that come to net during the last hour of daylight I know my journey home in the dark will be one of intense and glowing pleasure. Every roach angler who reads this will know exactly the kind of feeling I have failed to describe!

I could, if I so wished, almost certainly catch several roach well over 2 pounds in a season. All I'd have to do would be put in enough time on a water known to hold them, such as Startops reservoir at Tring. I'd have the advantage of knowing a number of people who fish there regularly and who have already done the spade work. All I'd have to do would be to follow their advice and instructions to the letter, bide my time, and eventually they'd come. There's a chance, too, that I might even get a 3 pounder, if I treated the project seriously enough and disciplined myself to behave like a carp-fisher; but somehow it doesn't feel right. I could sit a week and wait for a big carp, but when I'm roach-fishing I like simply to catch roach. I know that I, and most of my immediate friends, feel this way and while there's a certain amount of rivalry between us if we fish together, our main aim is to *find* and *catch* fish. What's more we *enjoy* asking someone to come and sit in on the fun. We are not confined to one spot. We can rove at will generally speaking (as could thousands of other anglers if they didn't confine themselves to the nearest comfortable swim) and if one of our number finds fish he doesn't hog them to himself but usually invites someone else to join him. I have known days when three of us have shared a swim hardly big enough for one man to exploit properly, and undoubtedly in the process we've probably caught fewer fish between us than one man could have caught on his own, but the important thing about it *was* the sharing. I believe that any angler can enjoy roach-fishing without becoming too deeply involved technically, and I leave special float-fishing techniques, aimed at extracting the last ounce from a swim, strictly to those who are more qualified to advise than I am. Those anglers who have to try and win matches must develop techniques to deal with the fish they find in their allotted space, and somehow they manage to catch them *despite* the noise and disturbance caused by spectators and other competitors. They do it by technical skill rather than by stealth and observation, and very often manage to extract incredible weights despite their obvious disadvantages.

It is often possible to march up in full view of the fish, to dump down a basket, to wave your arms, stamp your feet and still catch roach. I've seen it done, and were it not possible I'm quite sure there would be thousands fewer roach caught each season! But these things surely cannot help and I have no doubt whatsoever that more and bigger roach are caught by a cautious angler than by one who doesn't bother.

F.J.T. roach fishing with pike tackle made up in readiness

Choosing swims, recognizing conditions, preparing baits, deciding on methods and tactics, groundbaiting, presenting hookbaits and a hundred other factors have to be considered but one of the all time greats, the late Captain L. A. Parker, had this to say of roach. 'I do not think we pay sufficient attention to shadows. We all know they are there and we all know they scare fish but in our keenness to start fishing we forget.'

That, I regard as lesson number one.

## Observation

Locating the fish, or knowing where they are likely to be is the next natural step.

Some anglers are able to read a water correctly, assess the possibilities, set up suitable tackle, choose the right bait and begin catching fish almost immediately, irrespective of conditions. They have a little bit of magic other people do not possess and there's no way they could pass it on, even if they wanted to. These anglers are rare individuals, however, and though they may be complimented for their special skills they need not be envied too greatly. Most roach-fishing situations respond to common sense thinking and average fishing ability – which is just as well for had it been otherwise I'd still be wondering what roach looked like!

The more roach-fishing you do, the better you become at it, but there's no basic starting point. Learning roach-fishing is not like learning golf or fly-casting. You can be taught those and many other things by learning basic principles and, by practice, progressing, but it's difficult to decide just where to start, and what in fact comprises a basic roach-fishing principle! If there is one I don't know it, but I suppose the nearest to it, and the most useful first step, is to recognize that no one can catch a roach that isn't there either because it never was or because it's been scared away. That's an old cliché but it's sound. You must start off with the fish.

I think it's worth remembering that while some waters offer no real indication of the whereabouts of fish, others do. Those straight, characterless, canalized stretches of water are popular with match anglers because they are uniform, and because the fish are likely to be fairly evenly spread around, but there's very little you can learn from them by just looking. One swim appears to be just as good as another, and it takes practical fishing experience to discover the hot spots. I wouldn't know where to start looking myself!

Fortunately, however, many waters in the country still have some character left and it is possible to recognize roach swims because of certain characteristics. When you become involved in roach-fishing you begin to notice these characteristics and, later, you find yourself associating them with different styles of fishing.

It's impossible to lay down any hard-and-fast rules about how a roach swim should be chosen, but I would emphasize that it should be chosen for a reason. I don't think it really matters what the reason is provided it stems from observation. Even the condition of the bank could indicate the presence or otherwise of roach. Worn and well-trodden places at least suggest that those areas have been fished regularly and it's for you to decide then whether or not they're worth fishing. Whatever your decision happens to be, it should be made through observation, and although this may not be the best method of locating roach, it's better than sheer guesswork. Any observation, any plan (even a wrong one) is, in the long term, better than a chuck-and-chance-it attitude.

There are, of course, other ways of selecting a swim and the most important factor regarding roach shoals has to do with food. Roach tend to feed as a shoal, starting and stopping at around the same time and often their foraging habits tend to move the shoal around considerably. It is fairly safe to assume that roach frequent certain areas purely and simply for food, but there are times when comfort (or escape from discomfort) causes them to move around also. Thus it's possible to figure out locations by studying the set of the current, the presence or otherwise of plant life, available cover from predators and temporary respite from heavy floodwater in the form of slower-moving slacks and eddies.

When the water is low, for example, the shoal may be located in one spot and a rise in level may move them into another. You won't be able ever to say with certainty that 'the roach are here because . . .' but you will be able to say that 'the conditions *are right* for them to be here'.

The feeding habits of roach vary considerably from water to water and only observation can really provide the knowledge necessary to catch them consistently.

If you can say, for instance, that the roach in such-and-such a swim usually come on feed when the level is up, when it's slightly coloured, when it's beginning to drop, when the light's beginning to fail, or when the temperature is above a certain figure, it doesn't really matter that you don't know *why* it happens. What's important is that you've *observed* that it does, and that you're now able to take advantage of the fact.

Much of this information can only be gathered over a period of time by practical fishing but while it isn't possible to describe a typical roach swim, it is perhaps possible to suggest spots where they're *unlikely* to be found. And that helps considerably.

I do not for one moment suggest that everything here will apply to all waters. Of course it will not. But these generalizations often *do* apply. It is reasonable to say, for instance, that roach in slow-moving waters don't like to buck strong currents for long periods – and hardly ever in winter. In flood water they won't normally fight it out with the increased flow *and* the filth that's coming down with it. They'll seek somewhere quieter. When the water is thick and heavy they are more likely to be in a dead slack than at any other time – provided that slack is relatively clean. Eddies that move round in big slow circles when the water is high are often too turbulent to hold roach in low-water conditions. Clean-bottomed areas sometimes become filthy when flood debris accumulates; dirty areas are sometimes washed clear down to the gravel bottom after the first flood.

Observation in summer can also help locate shoals in winter; not necessarily in the same spots but possibly near by where the current is now similar. It doesn't always follow, of course, but it is always worth considering. Lily-pad holes in summer often hold roach in abundance and in many situations those lily-pad holes still hold roach in winter. The food supply, so important to their location in summer, is even more important in winter. The line of cast may be very different, the depth and range may have to be increased or decreased accordingly, but I believe it is reasonable to expect the roach to be fairly close to hand.

Clean, gravel-bottomed areas and gentle runs through bulrush beds are other good roach-holding spots and it's always worth remembering those clean-bottomed areas and marking them well for later in the year. Deep holes below shallow runs are excellent winter holding spots, but there are times when they are just that and little else. Holding spots – not feeding spots.

The battle is half won if you know the roach are there but, of course, you can never be sure. In summer you can *see* roach; in winter they're seldom visible. It's often like the 'chicken and egg'. You need to locate roach before you catch; you need to catch one in order to locate! Observation will eventually provide the answers, however, and almost certainly there will come a time when you begin to recognize roach swims and feeding areas that relate to different conditions. Springs and land drains put fresh water in a river, and if you know of one it may lead eventually to a roach shoal simply because it gives you a starting point. The train of thought should take into consideration the time of year and water temperature and the effect the influx of water is having. Will it attract roach or not? It could do either depending upon the situation and the conditions prevailing at the time. And without trying to confuse the issue, I have to try and make it clear what I mean. There are so many sets of circumstances, any one of which could swing the odds one way or the other. Let's look at a couple of them.

It is well below freezing, the margins of the river are fringed with ice and the water is as near to freezing point as it can be without actually solidifying, but the little spring is still running because it comes from below ground. It is putting *warmer* water (comparatively) into the river and (in my experience at least) this often brings about an accumulation of fish.

It is a very warm 'summer's-day-in-winter', the water temperature, after a long mild spell, is 45°F. The water in the spring is 39°F and it is having a *cooling* effect on the river where it enters. In my experience that tends to move roach *away* from the immediate vicinity. (In high summer, and the early part of the season too, it often attracts because of its cooling and oxygenating effect.)

Again I must emphasize that I'm not laying down rules; I'm suggesting that you *observe* such things. Then tie them up with what your plummet tells you about the bottom contours and try to figure it out yourself. You'll be wrong many times, but you'll also be right often enough to consider it worthwhile. And even if your thinking is all wrong, and you find the roach in situations completely contrary to your line of thought, it doesn't matter! That's just one of the real joys of roach-fishing.

Roach galore from Ireland

### Practicalities

I have left any mention of tackle, bait or fishing method until now because I believe quite sincerely that we all tend to pay too much attention to details of rod length, float pattern, shot size and other items of equipment *before* deciding where we are going to apply them.

I will leave the technicalities of sophisticated match-fishing and specimen-hunting to those who are more qualified than I am to discuss those particular aspects, but even simple, everyday roach-fishing demands a basic understanding of many angling methods. It is not easy to know where to begin but, for reasons of popularity, let us start with float-fishing and consider a pretty ordinary small-river roach swim. There are countless swims like it (or that have some of its characteristics) all over the country and it doesn't demand anything special in the way of tackle. It is below a wide bend where the river narrows slightly, runs fairly uniformly for about 6 yards and then shallows up slightly before it deepens again. In all it is about 15 yards long and 5 feet deep. The current strikes the near bank at the head of the swim and then sets diagonally across toward the opposite one; and it is nice and lively. To the immediate left, on the near bank, is an area of slacker water brought about by set of a current. If there are any fish in this slacker area the chances are that you'll scare them when you settle in and start to fish, but don't worry too much. If you *can* avoid it, do so, but for the time being concentrate on the run of the main swim and regard the slacker water as secondary. Keep it in mind though; it could be important later in the day.

I am always reluctant to suggest baits, because what's good for one water isn't necessarily good for another, but because maggots are most widely used and convenient, let us assume that you are going to use ordinary, white, good-quality maggots for most of the time. (But *do* take a loaf of bread with you when you set out! So few anglers seem to bother these days, but bread is still a super bait and really does catch better-quality fish in the long run.)

The choice of float to suit the conditions must be yours and yours alone, but a good rule of thumb (if there is such a thing) is to keep it as small as you can consistent with its ability to carry enough shot to get the bait down to the fish.

If the current is such that a one-shot quill or a little flat-top balsa will do – that's fine. If it's a bit faster, and you need more shots to keep the bait from being swept through too quickly, and too near the surface, you'll have to use a float with more buoyancy. And remember that in the general course of events this calls for a float with the buoyancy at the top to prevent those little swirls of current from pulling it under and registering false bites. I've used everything from turkey quills to modern wire-stemmed Avon floats to deal with similar swims and, of course, the modern materials and greatly improved design of the Avon float give it a slight edge over a quill.

Ask ten anglers how the float should be shotted and you'll get ten different answers, all of which, if applied with any degree of skill, could still result in roach being caught.

I do not know (perhaps because I know nothing of hydrodynamics) why it's possible one day to catch roach with the shots all bunched near the hook and on another to catch them with the shots evenly spaced. I've theories and ideas, of course, but without being able to watch what is going on below the surface there is no way of telling if I'm right. But I *am* sure of one thing. Roach don't *try* to pull floats under! They intercept food coming down with the current and the behaviour of the float depends upon how the bait is presented; how it is accepted by the fish, and how the shotting affects it. So, for the sake of simplicity, I'll suggest that the shots are evenly spaced below the float. Some experts may not agree, and you may well discover, by juggling them around, that the shots are better spaced differently. You may find that one large shot is better than two or three small ones. You may find that you get better bite registration by putting the last shot a lot nearer the hook. You may find a very tiny shot is better than a larger one in this critical position. You may find it helps to pinch a biggish shot directly below the float to stabilize it and make it cock much more quickly. All these refinements have to be decided by you, but for the time being I regard evenly spaced shotting to be adequate for most ordinary roach-fishing situations.

Loose feeding with maggots at the head of the swim can have several effects on the behaviour of the fish. It can cause them to drop back, move upstream or, occasionally, to swim deeper or shallower to intercept the feed. Timing is therefore important and obviously this is tied up with the amount of loose feed used. Each situation has to be judged individually and while it is sometimes possible to be spot on first time, it may take an hour or more to assess the situation correctly. The object, generally speaking, is to put the hookbait through the swim at about the same speed and depth as the loose feed. Negotiating a shallow spot in the swim calls for a holding back of the float at that precise point to allow the terminal tackle to rise briefly and clear the obstruction. This is easily executed in a swim of this nature because the tackle is proceeding in a straight line from where you're sitting. It's less simple when you're sitting at right angles and trotting down a couple of rod lengths out, but, again, this can be done with a stable Avon float.

Often, in a situation of this nature, the act of holding back induces bites, and one cannot be blamed for assuming that the loose feed has accumulated immediately above the shallow section and that the fish have gathered there too. It may well be so; but it may be that the fish themselves are at that level all through the swim.

I could go on with this theme for a long time and I could mention many situations where floats and tackles entirely different from those described are essential. But it would take a book – not a single chapter – and even then I'd be lacking!

I would like to suggest, however, that irrespective of how long you've fished the main swim with maggots, it's always worthwhile spending an hour in that near-bank slack or eddy. Feed it while you're fishing farther out if you like, but fish it nevertheless.

And, if you've a real desire to catch a few better-quality fish towards the end of the day, take the trouble to change tackle and tactics completely. An hour's 'laying on' towards dusk, using a bigger hook and a knob of paste or a cube of crust in the slower or slacker water, will not only provide a welcome rest from constant flogging with trotting tackle, it may very well produce the best fish of the day.

You could conceivably use the same float and, by bunching the shots, present the bait on virtually the same tackle, but I believe it is well worth while making a complete changeover to a bottom-end-only attachment. Bites are likely to be slower and more confident in these circumstances, and a glide-away bite will often be preceded by a 'flat-float' or 'lift' registration.

Not all swims are as easy to fish as this typical 'going-away' kind, however, and conditions can change so quickly in winter that even easy swims suddenly become difficult. Strong winds can make float tackle difficult to control, flood water can put fish off feed or move them elsewhere, and sharp frosts can put roach completely 'off' overnight. There comes a time when conditions are such that it pays to play a waiting game with the bait anchored in one spot for fairly long periods.

Roach in heavy floodwater, for instance, are hardly likely to chase small baits passing through the swim at a rate of knots. It's unlikely that they would see them anyway and while heavy floodwater does nothing to improve roach fishing, it does not always spoil it completely. One of the best roach I ever caught came from a floodwater eddy in January, and I have caught many better-than-average fish from similar spots over the years.

When you've been used to practising an active kind of fishing like trotting down for roach, and when you've learned to expect bites to come fairly frequently, it can be boring or frustrating having to sit it out and wait for bites in a floodwater eddy. But you will almost certainly encounter these conditions at some time or other and I believe it is as well to resign yourself to a less productive kind of fishing than to keep flogging away for nothing.

Anchoring a bait on the bottom does not mean it has to stay there all day without being moved. In fact, it should be moved frequently and the chosen area of water should be searched with a bait moved at intervals rather than with one that's continually on the move.

You can safely scale everything up in these circumstances and think in terms of fewer but probably bigger fish. Bigger baits fished on bigger hooks and heavier lines will probably produce just as many bites anyway and, in the event of a really big roach taking hold, the chance of landing it will be considerably increased. A 4 pound reel line and a No. 10 or 8 hook tied direct for use with baits like lobtails, breadcrust paste, or perhaps a bunch of maggots, may appear crude by many roach-fishing standards but it is perfectly suitable for this situation. One of my favourite ways of dealing with it is by hanging or 'stretting' quite close to my own bank.

I know of several mid-stream roach-holding swims where the fish merely move closer in during times of flood. All they've done really is move out of the main current into one that's more acceptable, and it's not at all unusual to find them tucked right in close to the bank.

Stretting (or to give it its full name 'stret-pegging' – where *did* that word come from I wonder?) means little more than hanging on in the stream below the tip of the rod. It's all tight line work and it is best practised with a float that's attached 'top and bottom' style. A float attached at the bottom end only tends to be pulled under continually by little fluctuations of current in these near-bank runs. The bait spends a lot of its time lying on the bottom but occasionally the current causes it to rise briefly (and often attractively). The float lies almost flat or at best half-cocked because the tackle is set a good deal

Ken Taylor stretting for roach, dace and grayling

deeper than the water. It could be described, I suppose, as laying on in a spot where the current is just that little bit too strong.

If you load the tackle with one large shot near the hook (6 inches to a foot), stick the rod in a rest and wait for events, you'll probably get bites but, if you let out a little line occasionally, lift the rod tip every so often and make the bait search the area downstream, the chances are you'll get more.

If you use tackle that is shotted evenly the bait will probably spend less time on the bottom than if it is held down with a single large one. In some conditions that may be an advantage, but when there's colour in the water due to flooding, I find most bites come when the bait is actually lying still. Nevertheless, I still think those occasional movements of the bait caused either naturally by the current or by rod-tip manipulation help make the method more interesting and more productive. And there are times when it becomes a fun-method too. If you happen to find a shoal of feeding roach holed up in a near-bank situation like this, you can miss a great many bites. Most come when the line is taut to the rod tip and are registered not only by a smart dive of the float, but also by a snatch on the rod tip. If you're holding the rod and just supporting the weight of it in a forward rod rest you may hit two out of three; but if you leave the rod in rests as we're all inclined to do when sport is slow, you'll be lucky to hit one out of four.

Sometimes an upstream bite slackens the line to register a perfect flat-float registration which is usually easy to hit, and occasionally there comes a memorable bite that takes place while the bait is rising in the water. These are often difficult to miss and at times the roach literally hooks itself. Much of the real pleasure I get from this particular situation comes from the number of *different* bites I get; and of course from the satisfaction of connecting occasionally in what I regard as challenging circumstances.

There are many situations, however, where simple float tackle is difficult to use and where, without a great deal of skill and knowledge, the swim would be better exploited with simple leger tackle.

Where the flow is too strong, casting range too great, or the bottom so uneven as to make float fishing difficult, a leger may make life a lot easier. The swim can be covered by rolling and bumping down and across with the current and the hot spots can be found by taking note of the line of cast. That's important! If you remember exactly how your last cast was made, the distance and angle involved, and if it results in a good bite, the chances are you can repeat it. Otherwise, there's a certain amount of guesswork involved until you hit the right spot again.

It would take reams of text to go into the details of legering for roach and it cannot be done here, but I believe the importance lies in knowing when the leger is indicated and having confidence in it as an alternative method.

There are scores of ways of loading a leger tackle, and in many situations it is sufficient to remove the float and simply bunch the existing shots. That is not always the *best* way, but it works often enough. The leger is supposed to be free-sliding, and the line is supposed to pull through the attachment, but, as already explained, in practice it seldom happens. In rivers especially, the lead usually moves with the bite. Hence the need for minimum loading. Remember – only enough lead to hold lightly!

Very often the amount of lead required to shot a specialized float is a lot more than would be necessary to hold a floatless tackle. Experiment with loadings by all means and do not expect the roach to come to the leger without extensive searching and careful groundbaiting. Remember though that you cannot actually *see* the path of the tackle, so try and figure out just how it will tie up with the groundbait.

Use any form of bite registration you like; that's a matter for personal preference, but if possible use one that allows you to hold the rod all the time. I still prefer to use my sense of touch because that's a part of roaching I truly enjoy.

One final point about the leger. Crust, paste and flake baits can be deadly in winter, but even small portions need a comparatively big hook, and I rate size 12 as the smallest. I've seen it tried, but there's no way you can leger a crust cube on a size 20. If you doubt my word, try it and see how long you can keep it on there!

# 12 Dace

I have spent a long time on many rivers fishing for dace. I don't
believe I have found out anything spectacular but I have had
reasonable success with these very pleasant little fish. I like them for
their spirit and enjoy catching them. I have never had a *really* big
dace. My best weighed 15 ounces and on the day I had at least six
weighing three quarters of a pound. But I have had large numbers of
nice dace ranging from 6 to 10 ounces from rivers as far apart as the
Wye and Avon, Ouse and Thames. And it's these good-average fish
which I am concerned with here.

There is one thing to be said in favour of the dace, that being its
willingness to feed under conditions of extreme heat and cold. Many a
blank day has been saved by the discovery of a shoal of dace.

The ways of catching them are legion, and they are liable to turn up
anywhere along the river and at any depth from surface to rock
bottom. They are reputed to be quick biters but I have seldom found
this to be the case when dealing with good-quality dace. Those tiny
dace weighing less than an ounce are indeed difficult to hook, but who
wants to hook them anyway?

Dace, as a rule, are lovers of the streamy well-oxygenated water,
but I have caught large numbers of dace in deep slack water. At one
time I used to think that they had moved from the streamy water
temporarily, due to some change in conditions, but now I know that
there are some dace which prefer the deeper slacks. They are always
there and their behaviour is exactly the same as the roach with which
they live.

Often I have fished these deeper slacks and found that due to very
cold conditions the dace have been the only fish willing to feed, but
under slightly warmer conditions I have had almost equal numbers of
roach and dace. At these times the bait has been either paste, flake or
crust fished on the bottom.

Dace, roach, chub and bream from the Ouse in winter

There have also been many times when I have caught dace on huge lobworms when I have been legering for chub. Make no mistake about it – a dace has no difficulty in getting a No. 4 hook in its mouth. No one wants to catch dace on No. 4 hooks of course, but it does rather go to disprove the idea that anything larger than 18 is too large for dace.

If I find that dace are in my usual chub swim and I am too lazy to move on in search of chub, I very often scale down the tackle to a No. 12 or 10 hook and leger for them with small crust cubes. I find this quite a pleasant form of fishing and it is most certainly excellent practice for more important kinds of legering. I have no doubt that I could catch three times as many dace if I used float tackle and maggots but I seldom bother to change over. I am soon bored.

During the close season of 1956 Richard Walker and I acquired a dead sheep from an obliging farmer. It had been dead a fortnight and we cut it into three sections with an axe, hanging each section over a favoured chub swim. I say 'we cut it up', but in actual fact the delicate job of dissection fell upon me – Walker was upwind lighting cigarettes and giving advice. He remarked at the time that those who considered specimen-catching a matter of luck should try their hand at this. The word, he said, should read 'pluck' and not luck. It was a gruesome business, but we had hopes of attracting large numbers of chub into

Fishing the wintry Ouse

the three swims and considered it worth it. In actual fact we did not catch a solitary chub when fishing time rolled round. These three swims were full of dace and both Richard Walker and I caught over thirty each in a couple of hours. All of them were good-quality fish, many were between half a pound and 10 ounces, and I have no doubt that had we fished on until darkness fell we could have doubled or trebled the number we caught. It would have been slaughter to keep it up and the fishing soon lost its attraction. What does interest me about the whole affair is that those three swims, for the whole of that year, became the best dace swims in the fishery.

Of course it isn't everyone's idea of fun cutting up dead sheep, and such ideas are only practical in the summer, but you can bait up a dace swim just as effectively in other ways.

One way is to suspend a tin of maggots over a swim for a week. A few holes have to be knocked into the bottom of the tin to allow the maggots to escape and if you do this at the end of your day's fishing instead of throwing all your remaining maggots in you will find plenty of dace there in a week's time.

Another way favoured by Richard Walker and me is to collect up all the spare bread at the end of the day and throw it into any reed or rush growing near to the swim. Do not soak it – leave it dry and throw it upstream if possible. During the week it becomes soaked and pulled to pieces by swans, moorhens, rats and various other creatures, but a large amount of it finds its way to the bottom of the river. We usually find that by the next week there are a lot of roach and dace in the area and we find that, the more regularly we do this, the less inclined the fish become to move out.

All this time I have been discussing the dace which prefer the quieter water and I think I can be safe in saying that anything which applies to roach applies to these dace as well, although each species often comes on feed at different times of the day.

The other dace – the occupants of the streamy water and more especially the shallows – are very different.

These are dace which fall to the dry fly, the dapped live fly, the chrysalis and almost any other bait floating on or near the surface. For the greater part of the year they live in water no more than a few inches deep, but in times of flood there is invariably a deeper slack nearby to which they retire.

Living as they do in shallow water, they are quite easily approached provided you are low down and near to the water. The appearance of anyone on the high bank above, however, sends them milling in all directions with fright. Even in the winter they are quite visible on the shallows, but are decidedly more difficult to catch than in the summer. A handful of chrysalids thrown on to the surface of the water and allowed to float downstream will often betray their presence. It is surprising how freely dace rise – even in the coldest of weather – *provided there is a little sunshine.*

To catch them in summer is easy. You just float a surface bait down to them on fine tackle – tackle that is not encumbered by float and leads – and unless they are preoccupied with one particular hatch of fly or an abundance of one particular form of underwater life, you will catch them.

Sometimes you will find them nosing among the growths of silk weeds, or in the algae growths on boulders or concrete piles near bridges, and then they are extremely hard to catch.

At other times you will find them feeding readily on one particular surface fly and, unless you can offer them a correct imitation or an impaled natural, you will be lucky to catch one at all.

I well remember one day in August when my brothers and I found a shoal of dace feeding on spent daddy longlegs. Our efforts to interest them in maggots were a waste of time and we decided to spend an hour or so collecting 'daddies'. We spent more time chasing about the field for the 'daddies' than we did actually fishing, but eventually collected enough for the last hour before dark. When we fished with them, however, we found that their bodies were so soft that the rising dace sucked them off the hook before we could strike. Then I hit on the idea of joining two No. 12 straight-eyed hooks together by the simple process of passing the point of one through the eye of the other. The 'daddy' was hooked on the top one and the bottom one caught the dace! After that we couldn't go wrong. A fairly strong breeze was blowing the daddy longlegs on to all parts of the river and I reached the fish near the far bank by using an empty bubble float a yard from my hook. The wind carried it over to the fish and the bait only was allowed to touch the water. I do not know how many we caught, but it must have been between fifty and sixty – and there were very few *under* half a pound.

We have watched them feeding in the same manner several times since, but on each occasion we have been more concerned with the large chub a few yards farther on.

While it is quite true that dace will show themselves to chrysalids in winter, it is not so easy to catch them on floating baits as it is in the summer.

Nowadays I do not bother to try. Having found my dace, I settle down in the nearest spot upstream where it is deep enough to use a float and keep trickling a little feed in at my feet. Maggots are the most deadly, of course. It takes quite a time, but eventually the dace move up to where the feed is going in. If you are using maggots for the job it is as well to watch the rate at which they are thrown in. If you put them in too rapidly the dace will move back after the ones they have missed, and if you put them in too slowly they will come up too close for comfort. Having got them interested there is no point in scaring them away every time you drop your float in the water.

If you can get a friend to creep downstream and watch the progress of the maggots and the behaviour of the dace you will be able to get the rate of introduction down to a nicety.

However, if you really want to catch dace in the shallows without the bother of bringing them up to you, you may find a use for the following tackle:

Take about 5 feet of fine monofilament and pass it through a 2 inch long piece of plastic fuel tubing (obtainable from any model aeroplane shop). Then heat a pair of pliers and pinch the tube at both ends. This will flatten the tube and make it watertight, but will still

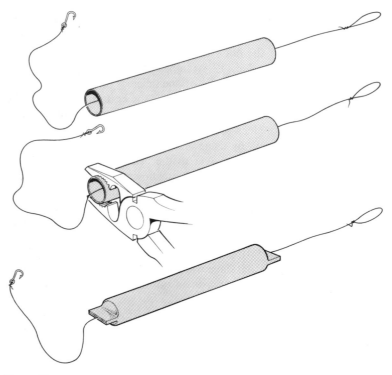

*Figure 17*

allow free movement of the monofilament. Then a hook at one end
and a loop at the other are the only requirements. Tie the loop to your
line and slide the tube up or down to the required distance (I think you
should leave at least a good yard between the tube and hook). This
float is almost invisible in the water and gives no indication of bites.
The bait must be watched as it floats down to the dace and if you are
using a chrysalis as bait – this is one time when you *should* strike
quickly.

Traditional trotting techniques using – say – a wire-stemmed Avon
float, are very productive in rivers of lively current. It takes time to
'work up' the swim introducing maggots, hempseed or casters
(chrysalids) and when every fish caught is the same as the last, there is
no pleasure in it for me. My experiences on the Avon, Stour, Thames,
Thame, and Windrush have all been very similar. Once the dace are

'going', bites can occur almost every trot through, and if I am able to achieve this I lose interest in the fishing. It is, perhaps, different on rivers like the Test where the dace are fewer and generally larger. The hopes of a pounder are ever present and I am then encouraged to continue. But I no longer have the inclination to work hard on a swim that I know is likely to yield fish after fish weighing less than 4 ounces apiece. That or nothing much at all. It *is* demanding of skill, and perhaps these days I do not have that skill. I believe, however, that to do something well it is necessary to enjoy it. And I've never really enjoyed mechanical repetition.

# 13 Rudd

The rudd has been considered a near-surface feeding fish and is associated with self-cocking floats and slowly sinking baits. I have caught lots of rudd in this manner and I usually find that for each fish I catch I have to add another 2 feet distance to my next cast. The more fish I catch, the farther they seem to drift away from the banks until they are at last quite out of casting range. Most of the rudd I have caught this way have been rather small and where small rudd abound it is difficult to connect with a big one. There are times in summer when you can see the rudd near the surface and by quietly approaching them in a boat it is often possible to pick your fish. An accurate cast is then often the only thing necessary.

For his size the rudd fights well, but there is no need for heavy tackle or strong lines in order to catch him. Unless you expect to hook your rudd in or near the marginal reeds, or unless you have to force your tackle out a long way to them a 2 pound BS line is quite strong enough. Popular hook sizes are 12s and 14s, and the most popular bait is maggots.

However, for summer rudd-fishing I prefer to wait until it is almost dark and then throw out a few crusts into the margins. Evidence of rudd will soon be seen or heard as the smaller ones set to work on them. A floatless, leadless tackle, carrying a piece of crust an inch square, cast into the vicinity will often bring about the downfall of one of the larger ones.

On still, sultry evenings rudd will often be seen taking natural flies on the surface. Small artificial flies, cast with orthodox dry-fly tackle, will catch the smaller ones with rapidity. I do not think that it really matters what the fly is, but towards dark I have had my biggest numbers on a Coachman. In order to catch any of the largest ones on a dry fly, I used to have a very large dry fly, the name of which I do not know, but which resembled a dandelion seed. It floated down like

Rudd of good quality can be taken on fly tackle

a piece of thistledown, was all fluff and small hook, and it accounted for a good many rudd of one pound and over. I think that any white fluffy fly will catch decent rudd if they are feeding at nightfall on natural flies, but as I have not fished in this manner for several years now I would not care to be dogmatic about it.

In summer, at dusk, and for about an hour after dark a large piece of flake fished hard on the bottom will often catch a few of the better specimens but I have never succeeded in catching many in one sitting.

To get the best out of rudd-fishing I like to fish for them in winter, and the rougher it is the better I am pleased.

I like to fish with the wind in my face (irrespective of depth) when the water is really choppy and lapping at the bank near my feet. The rudd is noted for the manner in which he runs off with the bait in summer, and during the winter he still gives a good bold bite.

Rudd in winter, especially in rough or cold conditions, are near the bottom and that is where they should be sought.

I have caught rudd in winter by two methods and two baits – legering with medium-sized red worms, and float-fishing with crust. Of the two I think that float-fishing and crust have been the most successful combination.

I use for this method a long piece of thin quill – 10 or 11 inches long – and one fixed swan shot to cock it. The quill is fixed at the bottom end only (as described in the 'lift method', *Figure 15*). I find that it does not matter how rough the weather or how strong the wind, this rig stays put perfectly. I fix the swan shot about 6 inches from the hook (which can be about size 10 or 8) so that the crust bait remains suspended about 6 inches off the bottom. The whole thing must look most unnatural to the fish but that is the way I catch plenty of rudd in the winter. I do not really know why rudd should take a bait presented in this manner in preference to one lying on the bottom, or sinking naturally. All I know is that it is so, and my brother and I experimented a lot with winter rudd before finally deciding that this was the best method on the waters we fish.

As a river fish the rudd is hardly worth specialization in England. Occasionally orthodox roach-fishing will produce an odd rudd or two, but in the main they are not numerous. I am surprised that there are so few rudd in English rivers and I am sure that the introduction of them into some of the slower-moving waters would prove beneficial to summer angling. The weather is seldom too hot for rudd to feed and many long, hot, day-time hours could be spent profitably fishing for rudd when nothing else was feeding, if only they were present in sufficient quantity. Many large lakes are grossly overstocked with

A big rudd goes back

rudd and with a little enterprise and work many of these could be transported to near-by rivers to the satisfaction of all concerned.

Remembering how disease has been spread from water to water by the transference of fish, however, I would be the first to insist that it be done under strict supervision and after due examination. Rudd are subject to all kinds of weird flukes and parasites, so re-stockings should be undertaken *only* when a completely clean bill of health has been presented.

# 14 Carp

So much has been written about carp in the past twenty-five years that this specialized branch of angling has become more popular than ever before. Carp are truly a challenge to any angler and demand more of his time, patience and knowledge than any other freshwater fish.

I have fished for the fabulous monsters of Redmire without success but I have seen fish there which would astound the majority of anglers. I am hesitant to say what the biggest Redmire carp weighs, but I know I have seen several upwards of 40 pounds and one of at least 60 pounds.

I have fished for the 'uncatchable' wild carp of Wotton also without success, but I firmly refuse to believe they *are* uncatchable. No fish is uncatchable if you are prepared to give up everything in order to catch it. (After the big freeze-up in 1962, when many fish were wiped out, only one carp was found dead at Wotton Lakes, so it would appear that they have gradually died out.)

I have caught the 'wildies' at Wadhurst Lake and I have caught double-figure carp at Woldale, and other waters.

I have caught plenty of smaller carp in various parts of the country and a few in my own district and I know of no fishing more exciting than carp-fishing.

Richard Walker's 44 pound record carp has made a 10 pounder appear insignificant, but I ask you not to be discouraged by it. A 10 pound carp is a wonderful fish and anyone who catches one is quite entitled to give himself a pat on the back. Never mind about 40, 30, or even 20 pounders, just ask yourself how many anglers in the country *have* caught double-figure carp. There are lots of anglers who have caught them in numbers, but there are plenty of really keen carp men who have not succeeded so far. Carp are hard to catch!

I do not propose to set out methods of catching carp in this chapter. Richard Walker has written on all the orthodox and unorthodox

Kevin Clifford, one of today's leading carp men, with a 12½ pounder

methods of carp-catching in *Still Water Angling*, and I cannot tell you anything about carp-catching without repeating his words and works.

I can only try to give you some idea of what your approach to carp-fishing should be and to convince you that despite what many anglers tell you to the contrary – life is *not* too short to go carp-fishing. My brother and I put in some *three thousand hours'* fishing for carp in Wotton Lakes without success, but we were far from discouraged. Years ago I found some dead carp in the Sawmills Lake at Wotton Underwood, the largest of which weighed 29¾ pounds. The majority of the members of the club were unaware of their existence and I had previously only seen one. I had been most positively broken on three occasions while tench-fishing and of course put it down to carp. I do not think I was wrong, but until the dead fish were found I had no idea that the carp there were so large. The one I had seen was about 15 pounds. After finding these carp, I wrote to Richard Walker, who was almost as pleased as I was, as it bore out what he had often said about carp living in various waters without anyone being aware of their existence. He sent some scales to Percy Austin who very kindly read them and sent the findings to me. Part of his letter was as follows:

> Thanks for scales from 29½ pound carp which were of unusual interest, not so much for the age as the manner of death. All the scales had partially obscured centres and had suffered erosion over a prolonged period – probably several months. Each scale carries about a hundred eruptions similar in some respects to the scales of some marine fishes. These eruptions, which appear like blunt stalagmites, are caused by excessive alkalinity – the reverse effect of acidity (low pH), which results in *pitting* and erosion of the ridges. An overdose of liming or infiltration of water from limed agricultural land could be a cause.
>
> The age is *19 years+* (or possibly 20+) and although growth rate was steadily falling it was still fairly good. As for spawning, I am sorry that most of the usual evidence has disappeared in the process of erosion, but from what little is still visible the fish has spawned frequently – if not annually.

This set me thinking and I was puzzled about the excessive alkalinity of the water. However I had samples analysed and they were found to be pH7, or in other words neutral. Then it dawned on me that in the previous October a field on the far side of the lake had been very heavily limed. The field sloped and consequently drained into the lake and this would no doubt have accounted for the excess alkalinity. The dead fish were found in April, and if they had spent the last few months in an alkaline water I thought that this pointed to the fact that they had probably hibernated over on the far side of the lake which would get the most of the lime drainage. Added to this was the fact that the water over on that side was never fished in the summer, was often very coloured and, although mainly thick weed, contained several patches of weed-free water. All this I thought pointed to the fact that carp frequented that side of the lake. B.B., author of *Confessions of a Carp Fisher*, says that carp will always occupy the side of a lake least frequented by humans. This I thought was the place to fish for carp and I would like to be able to tell you that the outcome of it all was a battle successfully fought with a monster carp. In actual fact my brother and I had one run between us in the season and the carp (for I cannot believe it was anything else) dropped my hen's-egg-sized piece of flake after running about five or six yards. Since then the far side of the lake is more fished and is frequented by tench. There are no signs of any carp being there.

I tell this story because that is how you must go about your carp-fishing. You must not expect to get a carp or even a bite every time you go fishing for them. You will fish for many biteless weekends and you must be prepared to do so. You must glean every little piece of information you can and try to pinpoint the places that the carp are likely to frequent. If you make a rough plan of the lake you hope to catch carp from, and mark the spot every time you see a carp and every time one is hooked by yourself and reliable friends, you will perhaps be able to boil it down to quite a small area. It is my opinion that many waters in the country contain carp although they are seldom seen and never fished for.

If you are in doubt as to whether your water contains carp there are a few things you can do to find out. A punt is of no use for actual carp-fishing but it is extremely useful for spotting them. If you paddle around the lake quietly you may learn something which will help you in your actual fishing. Apart from the possibility of disturbing an occasional carp, you may come across some indentations in the bottom of the lake. They are the shape of a pudding basin and are perfectly round. These are made by carp delving for food in the mud. A carp of 8 pounds would make them about 6 inches across and slightly less deep. Those at Redmire make them about 1 foot to 18 inches across.

You may also find 'runs' in among the reeds and rushes, and some of the rush-stems may be broken at the water line and looking like a felled tree. This is almost a sure carp sign. The water is often very muddy and stirred up in the vicinity. At times you will see patches of clear water in the shallows where the weed has come adrift and floated upwards. This also is often caused by carp routing in the mud near the weed roots. At Woldale and I think at Redmire, the carp actually eat the weed. In June Woldale Lake is covered with weed but by mid-July it has *all* disappeared.

If you want to know whether carp frequent the margins you can try the following procedure. Take about twenty large crusts (at least match-box size) and tie them to twenty pieces of cotton. Throw them into the margins – mark them with a tag of white paper but leave the ends lying on the bank. When you revisit them you will find that some of the cottons are left with no crust on. This is of course caused by small fish, such as rudd, whittling it away. If, however, both crust and cotton have disappeared you may conclude that a big fish has taken it and the big fish might well be a carp. Look out for swans and moorhens, if you try this however. If there is a place where you can see the bottom in water which is too deep for swans to scour the bottom, you can try putting a precise number of boiled potatoes in periodically and seeing if any of them disappear. Boiled potatoes will be immune from small fish – though it is possible that tench or bream would take the smaller ones. If you cannot find a spot to watch the progress of the potatoes you can try the same procedure as with the crusts. Throw them out on pieces of fine *cotton* (not monofil or strong thread because of the damage it may do to birds) leave them a few days pegged down and then see if they have been taken. While you are doing this, take the water temperature frequently and you may find the most suitable conditions for your particular water.

I shall not go into great detail as to what to do when you have arrived at some sort of conclusion. You must pick your spot and decide on the bait to be used. Cast it out on sensible tackle according to the size of carp you hope to catch, be patient and wait!

Very early morning is probably the most favourable time of course, but remember that a bait in the water can catch carp, a bait on the bank can't. Disturb your bait as little as possible. Don't get worried in case the carp can't see it – carp will find it in a foot of silkweed or if it's buried in the mud. Once it's out there, leave it out. If you are fishing say from 8 p.m. on Friday night until 8 p.m. on Sunday night, there is no need to take it out more than once – about

A small wild carp taken on a potato bait

noon on Saturday, when you should get some sleep for a few hours!

If you have a bite which does not develop into a decisive run LEAVE IT! A carp will often drop the bait and come back again later. If you strike and miss – it won't – nor will any of its friends! Above all, be alert by your rod all the time – it's when you leave it that you get the bites, but if you should be away from your rod when you get the bite – WALK to it. Don't run! Once a carp really takes the bait it seldom drops it, but it will if you stamp along the bank like a fairy elephant. Always leave the pick-up of your fixed-spool reel 'off' or coil a few yards of line on to a ground sheet if you prefer a centre-pin reel. You will by now be conversant with electric bite alarms, but if you use one be sure that it's reliable. Be sure that it will work in the rain as well as in the sunshine and if it doesn't – throw it away and use silver paper on the line. On your carp expeditions go with a good friend or two good friends and become 'group minded'. Develop an attitude which states that 'we are going carp-fishing and it doesn't matter who catches one as long as one of us does'. At night, if you want to sleep, take it in turns to watch the rods – two awake and one asleep. It's lonely at night and pleasant to have a friend to talk to through the long hours – and you may need some help quickly!

I have not fished at Redmire pool, home of record-breaking carp, since the early 1960s. For ten years I fished odd weekends and saw only two fish caught – a 20 pounder by Peter Thomas and a 26 pounder by Joe Taylor. Today the water is controlled by a syndicate of dedicated carp anglers who spend weeks at a time fishing for the species they love so well. They have been successful beyond dispute, but they too have known failures. Their techniques have involved extensive pre-baitings with particle baits such as sweetcorn, raisins, trout pellets, etc., and it is in this field that they have apparently been most successful.

I find this especially interesting in view of what I wrote in 1958 which is as follows:

Redmire is an extremely difficult water to fish. There are plenty of waters where it is harder to catch a carp because they are much larger and contain fewer carp. Redmire carp are individually harder to catch – by which I mean that it is easy enough to find the carp there and to put a bait where they are bound to see it. The actual percentage of 'takes' is very small indeed.

Redmire is a triangular-shaped pool of about three acres and has a dam at one end – shallows at the other. It is in fact a typical carp lake. Running down the centre is a channel about 11 feet deep. The water is gin-clear and gently moving all the time towards the dam. The shallows are thick with weed and the deeps are interspersed with tall slender stems of potamagetan. If you take a cupful of water from any part of the lake you will see that it simply teems with daphniae. It is what the aquarists would call 'strawberry jam', and it is small wonder that the carp are seldom interested in bread baits, when all they have to do is open their mouths at any old time to feed. At certain times of course, the daphniae are thicker than at others, and sometimes, according to the water temperature, they accumulate more in the deeper water, but at all times a great number of carp are preoccupied with daphniae. Others are preoccupied with bloodworms which they delve for day after day in the red-coloured mud. When I see carp in 2 feet of water, up to their gills in mud, with their tails literally waving in the breeze, completely out of the water, I begin to wonder just how heavy these monsters really are. There, within easy casting range, are feeding carp – unaware of my presence, and completely oblivious to anything I can offer them on a hook. You may well say 'why not use bloodworms?' Why not indeed? The only trouble is these carp are not taking one bloodworm – neither are they taking a bunch of them. They are sucking in huge mouthfuls of mud and blowing out what they do not want. Trying to catch carp on bloodworms is like trying to catch a cow in a field on a blade of grass!

The only carp which are caught at Redmire are the odd exceptions. The owner of Redmire is very keen on duck and wild fowl and he feeds those on the lake with bread almost daily, and occasionally – very occasionally – one of the carp discovers that bread is food. Then sooner or later he is caught, but it is not so easy as all that. They are still very wary about hookbaits – not so much because they are attached to a line but more because a hookbait differs just that little bit from a piece of unattached bread. Richard Walker, experimenting on this, emptied a bucket full of mashed bread over the side of the punt, watched it sink to the bottom and then dropped a hookbait dead in the middle of it. In the morning the whole bucketful of bread had been eaten but the hookbait remained! As I stated before, carp (especially Redmire carp) are hard to catch!

Perhaps one answer to the problem would be to tackle it in the same way as the preoccupied tench problem. A long-term baiting policy with baits of identical size, large enough to put on a reasonable-sized hook, might eventually cause the carp to become interested in them. Butter beans or some similar pulse vegetable would fulfil these requirements, but in order to compete with the natural preoccupation they would have to be used in vast quantities over a long period. Should the carp finally become interested (actually this would be another example of unnatural preoccupation) the angler would be at an advantage, due to the fact that carp would have to *pick up* the bait and not suck it down like soup.

Using dehydrated chip potatoes in May 1956, I distributed the equivalent of 112 pounds of parboiled potato chips into Redmire Pool. They reconstituted naturally in the water to fair-sized identical portions and I had great hopes for the third week in June. On arrival the carp seemed strangely absent – so much so that after three days we began to wonder if they had all died. On the night of the third day there was a strong smell of carp and we began to hope. Then at 3.30 on the morning of the fourth day it seemed that the lake exploded. The carp were spawning and to anyone who has not actually seen it happening it is very difficult to find words to describe it.

The shallows became a seething churning bedlam! Huge backs appeared out of the water, tails twitched and shuddered and the water became a muddy froth. Near to the bank huge carp of 40, 50 and 60 pounds agitated the water as they spawned! Farther out the shadows of more carp could be seen as it seemed they waited their turn to move in. So close were these great fish that they could be touched with a rod tip quite easily and they went about the business of spawning completely oblivious to anything else. We rowed a punt through them in order to get a better view and this put them down, but within five minutes they were back again. So it went on all day. Noisily they wallowed and splashed in the shallows, at times completely leaving the water, and when we left in the late afternoon they were still there – still spawning and still oblivious. We caught no carp in those four days but we witnessed a spectacle which I'm sure very, very few people in this country have ever seen before.

The extreme fertility of the water is no doubt the reason why the carp there grow to such a tremendous size. Cannot these principles be applied to other waters? I think they can. In various parts of England, carp enthusiasts are seriously restocking their waters with King Carp of the same strain as those in Redmire Pool. One particular group of anglers, owning two lakes, have set about this in a very practical manner. The smaller of the two lakes was netted to remove the small rudd and common carp it contained. Then the water level was lowered and the remainder of the fish were ruthlessly poisoned. While the level was still low the whole area was very heavily limed and left for several weeks before being allowed to fill up again.

Weeds and water lilies were then introduced and, within weeks, what had previously been a stagnant, muddy puddle became a luxurious pool.

It was then stocked with King Carp and at the time of writing this, within twenty months of their introduction, these carp have reached a weight of between 4 and 6 pounds. The growth rate of this strain of carp is quite fantastic and I see no reason why enterprise and enthusiasm should not create many other 'Redmires'.

Since those days I have spent much time in the USA, where I have fished for carp at every opportunity. My best fish, from Arkansas, was a common carp of 26 pounds. I fished very deep water and caught carp on such baits as chicken liver, fish guts, fish portions, bread and many mixtures containing scents and flavours including good bourbon whiskey!

I caught a double-figure fish at dawn one morning when the boat deck was covered in frost. I caught another that same day at three p.m. when the temperature hit 80°F. At depths of over 30 feet I am sure that water temperature changes very little.

I mention my American experiences for two reasons. One is that I think we should try using fish and meat baits more often. The other is that it has been proved over there and possibly to an even greater extent in the UK that carp-fishing does not necessarily end with the summer.

Nowadays I would say it ended on 14 March at midnight. It seems that carp-fishing has changed and so have carp-fishing attitudes. Every situation is different.

There are a few carp waters which go on producing fish until the end of October, and possibly a little later, if the weather holds fair. Others tail off at the end of September. Some waters are noted for their big fish, others, for their average-sized, fast-moving common carp. There are waters which have not known the meaning of the word restocking and the chances of a fish over 6 pounds are very remote.

These are the waters which, in the days just after the war, were the only ones available to anglers who loved to fish for carp. There was

F.J.T. wades out to net a carp hooked by Joe Taylor and badly weeded in the middle of the lake

something different about the carp-fishing then. A carp angler was either considered crazy or he was respected simply because he was prepared to devote so much of his life (some said life was too short to go carp-fishing) to the pursuit of what was then a mysterious and exciting fish. He *expected* his fishing to end in September. Now times have changed. Today we have waters holding 20, 30 and 40 pounders which are the results of stocking programmes calculated to produce just such fish. It's little short of amazing how carp have grown in very modest waters and if they'll carry on feeding it makes sense to carry on fishing for them.

Today we have groups of anglers who are dedicated to the capture of carp in winter. They say, and probably rightly, that no one caught carp in winter because no one tried before. Tradition had it that carp were summer fish, that they went to mud in the winter and were only re-awakened by the coming of warm weather. These hardy fellows report the capture of carp when snow lay thick on the ground, when ice fringed the margins of their favourite lakes and when their rod rings had to be thawed out to allow passage of line.

They report catching carp on a winter's night when the water temperature was as low as 36°F and they claim to have enjoyed it! I am sure they did, and that they will continue to do so. This is dedication and a real resolve to prove that traditional methods are not necessarily 100 per cent right. I, too, enjoy night-fishing in winter but somehow I do not want to fish for carp then. Cod from the pier and occasionally pike from the boat-house – yes. I freeze to death slowly but I *think* I enjoy it.

For real carp-fishing pleasure, however, give me the old-fashioned summer style, the old-fashioned lakes and the old-fashioned fish. I have been more deeply involved than most regarding the introduction and movement of carp stocks. I have enjoyed every moment of it and, at present, I am still waiting to see what three years of feeding has done to the 300 babies I introduced in 1976. Eighty yearlings introduced to an old canal some years ago produced seventy-three fish up to 14 pounds four seasons later.

I still recall the days when wild common carp were our quarry, however, and I find that waters holding such fish are still enchanting. There's an air of magic about them, but it ends for me when the summer has gone.

# 15 Grayling

As a coarse fisherman of reasonable experience it is understandable that I should come into contact with the occasional grayling. I have taken them from rivers as far north as the Tweed and as far south as the Avon; and I have been pleased to do so. I have eaten grayling and trout from the same frying pan and I have been hard put to decide which had the better flavour. I have enjoyed the peculiar but determined fight of the grayling and I have rated it highly. Most of the grayling I have caught have been taken when I was trotting maggots for dace, roach or chub. They have been accidental, but nevertheless very welcome catches. But because they came by accident I can claim no credit for their capture. The fact that they fell to maggots fished on float tackle in fast water simply provided further proof of the efficiency of accepted grayling-fishing methods. Who would dare to suggest that there is a more efficient method of bait-fishing for grayling than long trotting with the well known 'bob' and maggots? As far as my experience was concerned there was no other method worthy of consideration – with the exception of fly-fishing. But I was to learn differently during the winter of 1964-5.

Opportunity came for me to fish a southern chalk stream for coarse fish. Roach and dace were present but they were very easy to locate. Grayling, however, were fairly widespread and, while not easy to catch, they were more consistent feeders than the roach and dace. I believe that for the purposes of this chapter it will be better to describe my experiences with them instead of trying to tell the reader 'how to do it'.

I caught a fair sprinkling of these grayling by orthodox grayling-fishing methods but the majority (and the score was fairly high over the three-month period) fell to methods which I regarded as very far removed from accepted grayling procedure.

For a start the best-quality fish fell to bread and paste baits rather

Grayling

than maggots. And despite many hours fishing with worms and brandlings, no grayling fell to this bait at all.

Nevertheless it was not the choice of bait that intrigued me, but the rather unorthodox methods of their capture.

I have a great liking for roach and believe that to catch a really outsize specimen in such waters demands an approach which is different from the normal one. My approach, largely influenced by a roach angler of greater experience, was to leger with fairly large pieces of breadcrust and to feed the swim sparingly with a good-quality groundbait. The first fish taken on a bait presented thus in very fast water was a grayling of nearly 2 pounds. Others followed and eventually it became apparent that in some stretches of the river there was an area of *comparatively* slower water near to the bank. By 'near' I mean 6 inches to a foot – no more. This was usually noticeable where the banks were vertical and the river of uniform depth and speed of current. Long straight stretches of fairly even flow were ideal for the method in question.

The object was to use a somewhat lighter than normal leger tackle and to let the bait roll in until it was virtually touching the near bank, but at the same time fishing deep. It appeared that many grayling rested in this narrow area close to the bank. The tackle was arranged so that the bait wavered up and down in the current on a long link. The rod was poked no more than a foot over the water and I found myself sitting back some 3 yards from the water's edge. The advantages were twofold. The bait rolled into the bank much more readily and I kept out of sight of the fish. Even on a water so little fished I found this question of concealment to be most important.

Because of the speed of the current I walked some 30 yards upstream every time I introduced the small quantities of groundbait. I dropped it in at my feet and hoped that it would be somewhere near the bottom when it reached the baited hook area. I cannot be sure I was right, but I took enough grayling to make me think I was.

Later I fished maggots in the same manner but used a swim feeder to bait the swim. The grayling I caught were generally smaller and after several days at this I looked for signs of fish elsewhere. I had become fascinated by grayling and thoroughly enjoyed catching them, but I wondered if there might be a haunt where the roach and grayling mixed: and I went looking for a new pitch.

I tried several and caught grayling from them all but only in ones and twos. Several times I passed by an eddy on a sweeping bend and noticed that there was an area of almost dead slack water. Because of the nature of the river I ignored it, feeling quite confident that I should not find fish in it. One does not normally expect to find many fish in slacks on fast southern rivers, especially if those slacks are no more than 2 feet deep and the banks are hard with frost! But again I was to learn differently.

There came a day when an icy wind blew and carried with it rain and hail sufficient to deter all but the hardiest of winter anglers. I was not very keen to walk along the exposed banks and kept close to an old fishing hut which provided the only shelter for miles around. I didn't fish because I have now reached the stage when I no longer want to catch fish despite conditions. It is important to me that I *enjoy* my fishing and I was not *going* to enjoy fishing in such weather. Later in the day, however, when the rain ceased, I made some sort of a show. I put up a tackle and dropped a maggot-baited hook into this shallow slack which was but a few yards from my shelter. It was only a gesture on my part: to say that I had fished. I chose the slack because I could put my rod in the rest and watch the float without having to do any serious work. I set the tackle deep and 'laid on'. Each time I retrieved it, it was covered in weed, but I was not particularly worried; I did not expect fish anyway. After a time I set the tackle shallower and simply let the bait dangle beneath the float. Occasionally the wind would catch the float and move it around. Sometimes it would drift to the edge of the main current and be swept round gently back into the slack again. And there it remained for over an hour. When it suddenly dived under and disappeared completely I was astonished – and much too late to do anything about it! But I was stirred to try again. That was when I began to learn something about *losing* grayling. I caught two that day and lost four more. One of them, which I saw clearly and distinctly, was undoubtedly a 3 pound fish. It shed the hook after a few minutes like the other three. I should have realized, of course, that my hooks were too small. Having gone over to float tackle I was using small whipped hooks about size 16. My leger hooks had been size 10 and I had not lost any fish when using those. But size 10 hooks look indecently large on fine float tackle and I wasn't quite sure what I was doing wrong. I wondered if I was playing the fish too hard or if indeed I was not playing them hard enough. The peculiar 'propeller'-like movement of a hooked grayling has been the subject of much discussion. Do you use larger hooks and a bit of 'stick' or small hooks and great care to land big grayling? I had received advice of both kinds and still wasn't sure.

I wrote eventually to Eric Horsfall-Turner who has a much wider experience of grayling-fishing than I, and asked his opinion. He offered nothing in the way of advice but sent me some of his own grayling tackles to try. They were simple spades about size 12, tied to nylon monofilament of about $3\frac{1}{2}$ pounds breaking strain. I used them, and others like them, from then on and I don't remember losing another grayling! Since then the small shallow slack has yielded a great many grayling and a few dace and roach. It has become known already as 'Fred Taylor's hole'. From it have come a good number of grayling in excess of 2 pounds with 2 pounds 6 ounces as the best. They have been taken on paste crust and maggots simply 'dangled' in the slack; sometimes only a few inches below the surface, sometimes just touching bottom. At no time have I had to trot long distances for them and I cannot remember ever failing to get a fish from it.

Undoubtedly my best bags have come when the weather has been pleasant. Grayling will feed when it's so cold that nothing else will, but in my experience, limited though it is, they are more likely to feed in milder conditions.

F.J.T. unhooks a Test grayling

It was particularly noticeable as the winter wore on that failing light conditions tended to make the grayling more active. This, I understand, is often typical grayling behaviour, and in this respect they are very similar to roach in many waters.

Since then I have fished for them in the early hours of a summer morning and caught them with a fly in various conditions, but I have a lot to learn. It's a long time now since any fishing has interested me, confused me and made me swear as loud and as long as my newly found grayling-fishing has. I have learned a little about them and I have a healthy respect for them despite the fact that they are considered to be vermin in many waters. I hope I have the opportunity to learn a lot more, for they are well worthy of the effort.

The 'grasshopper' described and used so adequately by the late J. H. R. Bazley was a deadly lure for clear-stream grayling. It was, roughly speaking, a weighted hook bound with yellow wool. There were, of course, many variations, but it was used completely unbaited and its action, an up-and-down movement, teased the grayling into taking.

In fact, it was used in exactly the same way as the jigs described in the perch chapter! A forerunner of the US jig, or a copy? It matters not the slightest. Jigs in pink, yellow, black, black-and-white, and orange variations will catch grayling. You have my word on it!

# 16 Pike

If you wish to learn how to impale an unfortunate roach or dace on to a snap tackle without killing it, and how to hurl it 30 or 40 yards out into a lake, there to struggle vainly to avoid the death which must surely come to it in one form or another, then you need read no more of this chapter. I have in my youth and ignorance performed the above-mentioned ritual many times and each time I have shuddered, as did the unfortunate roach or dace as the hooks went home. I have since learned that livebaiting, far from being the best method of catching pike, is unnecessary on *any* water.

There are occasions, however, when a large pike can be seen and it is obvious that it is only necessary to drop a bait in front of it in order to catch it. In these circumstances I consider it excusable to offer it a livebait. Rightly or wrongly, the whole process is only going to take seconds and this form of livebaiting is vastly different from that which I have just described.

I have no great liking for the pike. I respect it as a good fighting fish. I cannot honestly regard it as beneficial in any water. I have been involved in arguments for and against the preservation of pike and I can only reach one conclusion and it is this. If you want pike for pike-fishing you are entitled to have them, but I believe you must seriously take into consideration what effect this will have on the other species. It is said that pike will kill off sick fish, thin out the small ones and maintain a balance of nature. This is probably true – in parts – but is nature's balance the balance for which we, as anglers, are striving? I think not. I believe we want to *improve* on nature and maintain greater and better stocks of fish. And this means that we must *consider* the question of pike removal very seriously. There is no quick answer. Each water must be judged separately and in accordance with the wishes of the majority of its anglers.

It is not possible to exterminate pike, and those who fear that they

F.J.T. with his 32 pounds 2 ounce pike taken from the River Erne in Eire

will become extinct if they are continuously removed need have no fear. The trout angler who stocks his water regularly quite rightly desires the removal of all pike from his water. He wages war on them and removes them by fair means or foul until one would think that under such an onslaught they would become extinct. What usually happens is that the numbers increase! The larger pike are killed off, of course, but the smaller ones, being more difficult to snare, shoot or gaff, and having none of the larger members of their family to keep them down, gradually increase in numbers. They eat lots of small trout and food which would otherwise be eaten by the trout and it's just possible that they still do as much harm to a fishery. But it can truthfully be said that at least the stock fish which are introduced each year are safer because of this unceasing war on the pike. This is what the trout angler sets out to achieve. It is right that he should do so.

Pike in rivers containing only coarse fish have a much better bargain. Size limits prevent the removal of smaller pike, local club rules often mean their preservation, and in many parts of the country it is forbidden to fish for pike until October. Size limits and preservation are very good things, but why it should be considered unsporting to catch pike before October I cannot understand. The pike is among the first coarse fish to spawn, and by June, far from being an unworthy opponent, is in absolutely tip-top condition. It has had three months in which to spawn and recover (assuming that it did not spawn *before* 14 March), and those three months have provided it with more food than it is likely to get in any other three months of the year. I have no desire to fish for pike in summer as I feel that tench and carp are more worthwhile quarry, but those that I have caught have given me the very devil of a fight. I cannot truthfully say that about pike which I have caught in February and March. The females have been bloated with spawn (2 pounds in an $8\frac{1}{2}$ pound fish is one example), and the males have been limp and lifeless.

The preservation of pike in coarse-fish rivers is not *always* advisable even for the pike-fishing. I will give an example of what I mean. Some friends and I rent a stretch of a narrow river. For a large part of the year it is choked with lilies and rushes and reed mace, and the water is very clear, but it holds some remarkable fish for so small a river. I spend a lot of time watching fish in this river and I have seen *very* large chub, roach and perch there in the summer. I have, however, *never* seen a large pike and this would appear strange, when I tell you that many are caught there upwards of 15 pounds in the winter. What actually happens is this. Towards December, the pike from the wider downstream reaches make their way up to the narrower, rush-filled stretches prior to spawning. We call them 'intruders' and indeed they are. They are out of place on such a small river, and play havoc with the large roach and even a 3 pound chub is not immune from their attentions. I watched a 14 pound pike swallow a 10 ounce dace there in one gulp and wondered how many such pike this small river could maintain and for how long? In view of these facts I think it is

If gaffed correctly pike suffer no harm

advisable to remove or destroy any large pike in the smaller rivers, especially those containing a good head of fair-sized other coarse fish. It is difficult to decide what *is* a large pike, and as a line has to be drawn somewhere I think that a size limit of 10 pounds should be adhered to and that all pike over 10 pounds should be removed. Smaller pike are an asset on a water such as the one in question as they do tend to keep the small fry and minnows down to a tolerable level.

There is one type of water where I think pike might well be retained and that is the vast still-water fishery. There nature often tends to make a better job of the natural balance of fish and food. Small fish breed with less interference than in a river and there are no great intruders to upset things. Pike are often the only fish worth pursuing in winter in a still-water fishery and as such provide good sport for the angler who prefers the lake to the river.

Having said a little for and against the destruction of pike – let us see how we can go about the business of catching them.

Pike-fishing can be divided into two main groups – i.e. mobile and static – and both methods can be practised in still or moving waters. Mobile pike-fishing means that the angler searches for his fish, covering a vast area of water with artificial baits, spoons or dead natural baits. Static pike-fishing means purely and simply the casting of a bait into a suitable swim and awaiting the pike's pleasure. The most popular method is of course livebaiting.

It is difficult to say which is the most productive type of angling. The livebaiters swear by their 'big baits for big fish' and the spinning enthusiast will produce a long list of large pike caught on small spoons just to prove them wrong.

## Mobile

Dealing with the mobile method first, I like to spin with all types of spoons and plugs, and I enjoy fishing deadbaits on various wobbling or spinning tackles. Each method seems to have its day and in order to obtain the best out of pike-fishing I think it is necessary to carry a considerable assortment of baits and tackle. I am quite aware of the fact that when a pike is on the prowl in search of food, it doesn't really matter what you offer it, but there are days when (as in trout- and salmon-fishing), a change of lure will often work the oracle. I have known occasions when a natural bait spun or wobbled was ignored by

F.J.T. spinning on a small Scottish loch

a lethargic pike, but a small spoon with a violent action was immediately taken. Taken all round, I think that a natural deadbait such as a small rudd, roach or bleak is more deadly than all the fancy artificials and striped horrors found in the tackle shop. The mounts cost very little to make, and can be made up of single-strand alasticum wire which is very pliable and not prone to kinking. A few eyed treble hooks, some whipping silk or thread, and a spot of cellulose varnish are all that is needed to make a variety of first spinning mounts. There is no need for fancy spinning or wobbling vanes as in my opinion these only destroy the natural action of the bait. An attractive wobble or spin can be given to any deadbait merely by adjusting the tackle to produce a suitable bend in the bait. Nevertheless I am convinced that spins and wobbles are not necessary when using deadbaits. The old-fashioned, but remarkably effective, Jim Vincent method of deadbait-fishing is, in my opinion, the most deadly of all, especially in still waters. There is no ironmongery required on the tackle, a short wire trace and one large treble being all that is required. The trace is threaded through the vent of the dead fish and out of its mouth and it is then attached to the line by means of a small swivel. The swivel is actually unnecessary as the action of the bait does not link the line but it is a safeguard against the wire trace cutting the line.

The old exponents of pike-fishing will tell you to retrieve slowly when spinning *any* bait, though I have yet to learn how to retrieve a heavy spoon slowly in shallow weedy water. Using the Jim Vincent method, however, you *cannot* retrieve too slowly, a half turn of the reel every thirty seconds is often enough. The bait should be cast into likely-looking spots and allowed to remain completely still for a few seconds. It will then begin to sink, oh so slowly, for all the world like a dying fish – turning and glistening attractively as it does so. A quick half-turn of the reel will cause it to right itself and another couple of turns will start it on its way back. A pause and it will begin to sink again, until another quick half-turn rights it once more. This action is very detailed and the most natural-looking I have ever used. There is no need to hurry – the longer you can keep the bait out there the more chance you have of hooking your pike. I would say that, apart from floating plugs, this is the only 'spinning' bait which can be used in shallow weedy water, and if it is intended to fish such water, it is as well to be careful not to prick the swim bladder when threading the bait. The weight of the trace is, as a rule, just sufficient to cause the bait to sink slowly, but if you prick the bladder it will sink too quickly for an efficient slow retrieve. In deeper water, of course, the swim bladder must be punctured to keep the bait deeper in the water. It is possible to incorporate lead for this purpose, either on the trace, or inside the bait itself, but I have never been able to do it without seriously affecting the action of the bait. The one drawback with this method is the effective fishing range. Without the use of lead, it is often difficult to cast long distances, but on the whole, long casting is seldom necessary. The bait is best fished in the margins. Cast along the bank as near to the margin as you dare, and as I said before retrieve very, very slowly. There will be no mistaking the strike, but immediately you get one, slacken off! This, if you have been used to using spoons and devons, etc., will be quite a job to get used to, but it will pay in the long run. A pike will not often release a deadbait once it has taken it, and you may as well give him a few seconds to get hold of it properly before sending the hooks home.

After you have been using a bait threaded in this manner you will find that the treble may become embedded into the fish rendering it ineffective. When this happens the continued strain of casting eventually tears the bait until it becomes useless. In order to combat this I usually employ a small, half section of plastic tube which fits snugly round the vent of the bait. A small bead prevents the treble from pulling through and keeps the bait in good condition for a much longer period. The bead also keeps the treble away from the bait and makes for more positive hooking.

I do not know how right I am in this, but I feel sure that in still water a pike hunts more by sight than its relative in the river. In my experience, a vibratory spoon is far more effective in attracting pike in rivers than it is in lakes, and I have seldom found the Jim Vincent method very successful in rivers unless it is fished in a special way. I said that a vibratory spoon will attract pike in rivers and that is quite true, but very often the pike will follow the spoon and eventually turn away having found out that it isn't all that it should be. This happens very often when the water is low and clear. Having seen this happen several times on such a day, I wondered if a deadbait would not be more successful so I spun one for some time without success. A change back to the vibrating spoon moved two more pike from out of the rushes but they did not take. That evening I prepared a few vibratory spoons for use the following day. I painted them a dull green hoping to make them invisible to the pike, and in the morning I fished a deadbait with a dull green vibrating spoon 2 feet up the trace (*Figure 18*). I caught seven pike that day, including four over 10 pounds, all on deadbaits! I am convinced that the vibrations of the spoon caused the initial attractions, and that the pike took the dead-baits when they found them to be real fish and not lumps of metal as on the previous day. In all instances the bait was cast downstream. The current gave the spoon maximum vibrations, the retrieve was very slow and the action of the deadbait was most realistic. This is not an isolated case and I have used it many times since with a fair measure of success. These small vibrating spoons however, are very deadly for

*Figure 18*  Deadbait attached 'Jim Vincent' style, plus small, uptrace, camouflaged, vibrating spoon

normal river piking. They are very easy to make by pouring some plumber's metal into an old spoon and letting it set. You are then equipped with a mould over which you place a piece of suitable metal cut to a 'leaf' shape and tap it to the required 'bend'. There is no need for extreme accuracy in cutting the metal and it is very interesting to cut various shapes and sizes and experiment. I have found that a piece of copper sheet which has been 'tinned' all over with solder is about the best metal to use. Aluminium has not enough 'body', so to speak. Having shaped your spoon it only remains to bore a hole in the wide end and mount it on a wire 'bar' (cheese wire is ideal for the smaller spoons) and equip it with an appropriate-sized treble hook. A bead and a lead shot or a piece of plastic tube on the bar will prevent it slipping down too far and will allow it to revolve freely.

You can vary your spoons by painting the inside red, or by tinning one side of the copper only. Silver and copper is a very old combination of colours for pike spoons and it is a very good one too.

You can also cut other types of spinners out of your sheet copper and try them with various colours and tail attachments. There is a lot of fun to be had on a dark winter's evening and a lot of pleasure to be gained from catching a pike on a lure you have made yourself. Whatever type of lure I make for river piking, I like it to have a really good vibratory action. I like to be able to *feel* it vibrating right through to the rod handle when I am retrieving. I think that this is the whole secret of spinning in rivers.

All this talk of making lures may appear to be miserly, and may give the reader the impression that I begrudge the cash to buy good-quality lures, but this is not so. I make my lures to suit the waters I fish and all the pieces are interchangeable. I can vary the weight of them to a split shot's difference and this is important on rivers such as I fish, where due to mills, etc., the current varies from hour to hour. I also fish more confidently and take more chances with a lure I have made myself but if I were to compare the cost of a shop-bought lure with one I made myself, and took into consideration the price of materials and *time involved*, there would be very little saving in it. However, as I have already stated, it can be a lot of fun.

The only other type of mobile pike-fishing is plug-fishing. I have used plugs quite a lot and in some respects they have an advantage over other spinning lures. Floating plugs can be used in shallow weedy water where heavy spinners cannot, but in any case I still prefer the natural bait. They can also be floated downstream on rivers where overhanging trees prevent accurate casting. They can then be retrieved after they have reached the point to which they would normally have been cast. This is a distinct advantage and a floating plug is the only lure with which this can be done. These small advantages and the fact that, again, no lead or anti-kink vanes are required, make the plug an item of equipment which no pike angler should be without. With a little patience and paint very efficient plugs can be made out of a piece of beech dowelling bored through the centre with a fine drill. There is no need to delve too deeply into the making of them; it is only common sense, and once again extreme accuracy is not necessary

### Static

Quite often the very act of fishing for roach will bring pike into a swim. The continued use of maggots and groundbait will activate the roach and this activity plus the disturbance caused by the occasional landing of fish often causes a near-by pike (or several pike) to take an interest in what is going on. I remember several occasions when big pike have been lifted out of the water when their teeth have become caught in the mesh of a keep net full of roach.

It follows then that if pike can be such a nuisance in a roach swim, the best way to catch them is to go roach-fishing! Set to work on the roach swim, but have a pike rod and tackle set up ready for instant use the moment a pike puts in an appearance. Often it is enough to lower a livebait on to a pike's nose. Sometimes it is necessary to anchor it out in the stream for a few minutes and this can be done on a simple leger or paternoster tackle. (See *Figure 19*).

If a float is considered necessary, it doesn't have to be a gaudy red bung and it doesn't have to be loaded down with loads of spiral leads

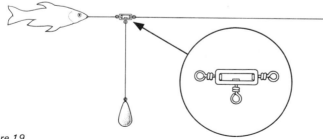

*Figure 19*

and other ironmongery! A piece of barrel cork or a wine-bottle cork, depending on the size of the bait, is much less conspicuous. A swan shot or two, again depending on bait size, is all the lead you need. And you don't have to stick trebles into the bait. If you choose to use a small one it is sufficient to lip-hook it on a No. 4 single (*Figure 19*). Allow a little longer for the bait to be taken when using this method and strike with a sideways pull. If you should not catch any pike the bait can be released after a short time none the worse for its experience, but it is seldom necessary to keep baits out for very long. One knows immediately a pike enters the swim and once this is ascertained the bait is usually taken very quickly.

You need a wire trace for this fishing, of course, but it doesn't have to be a hawser. A single strand Alasticum wire of about 10 pounds breaking strain is enough. Used in conjunction with a line of about the same strength (more or less depending on the size of pike expected) it should be able to deal with almost any pike you are likely to encounter. I'm always rather puzzled by the attitude of 'fine tackle' anglers who tell me I'm unsporting using a 6 pound line to catch a 4 pound chub, and who then go pike-fishing with lines of over 20 pounds breaking strain. They usually catch pike weighing about 4 pounds too!

I am convinced that livebaiters would catch more and better fish if they scaled down their tackle considerably and did away with their heavy leads and huge bungs.

### Catching livebaits

However, before we can livebait we first have to catch the baits and this is not always as easy as might be expected. Most anglers know a few places where they can always collect livebaits enough for a day's fishing. These places are usually still waters which are over-run with small roach and rudd and which will produce fish even in the worst conditions. These over-stocked waters are the Mecca of many livebaiters and often provide unlimited stocks for those who sell livebait throughout the winter. No special skill is required to catch them; a little cloudbait and a few maggots are usually all that is necessary. Nevertheless, I have known occasions when it has taken far too long to catch a dozen livebaits.

I've seen tackle used which just wasn't suitable for catching small fish quickly. Hooks as large as No. 12 and lines of 4 or 5 pounds breaking strain will catch them occasionally, but extra-fine tackle and tactics are usually required in order to catch them consistently.

Fine lines are not necessary to deceive the fish into thinking that they do not exist; they do, however, let a small bait behave more naturally in the water. For this reason I believe it is essential to use the finest possible link between the hook and the float. No big fish will be expected and even a 1 pound BS line will lift a livebait-sized fish.

Fine lines will not set bigger hooks as well as they will set the tiny Nos. 18 and 20 of the matchman, and I believe that even among unsophisticated fish the size 20 will take more consistently.

. I noticed this myself once when catching livebait on the River Kennet. Until I lost my last No. 14 hook I was content to use this size. Then the next smallest I had was a French spade-end tied to very fine link. It was size 20; and after that I seldom missed a bite. I was catching livebaits for a party of four and needed, I thought, about fifty of them. I caught them in record time on my tiny spade-ends.

I consider No. 20 to be the ideal hook size for livebaits in still waters, and while I can still catch them on larger sizes, I don't consider I'm well equipped without them.

Catching small roach and rudd in cold weather is not always easy and quite often the bites are so delicate that they're extremely difficult to hit. Correctly balanced tackle will help here. The recognized choice of terminal tackle is a tiny crow quill or porcupine, cocked with one small shot. Perfectly adequate as a rule, but there are times when a larger float, cocked with three or four BB shots is better. If the larger float is shotted right down to the last quarter-inch it will react beautifully to quick-biting small fish; and its extra weight will help if the fish are a long way out.

Shot positioning and depth can be important even among hungry rudd and roach and it pays to experiment with both if no bites are forthcoming. Even in the same water, shot positioning can vary from day to day. Sometimes the shot has to be down near the hook; sometimes it has to be touching the float and making it virtually into a self-cocker. The effect this sort of thing has on the bait is obvious. I experiment until I've found the set-up which produces most bites.

A combination of cloudbait and maggots seems to be the best answer as far as baits are concerned. A small, walnut-sized knob of cloudbait around the float every two or three casts will keep the fish in the area. Sometimes it's best to throw in the cloudbait first and then drop the baited hook into the cloud which forms. Half-a-dozen maggots thrown in loose around the float from time to time will help, too. And, of course, on some well-fished canals, the same tactics using hempseed instead of maggots are very deadly.

Very often, however, it's not always possible to go to one place for baits and to another for pike. Sometimes you have to catch the baits where you're going to pike-fish, and on a river this can be a problem. I can't speak for all rivers, of course, but I know that if a pike appears in my roach swim on any of the small rivers I fish, I can't get a bait for love nor money! At least, not a roach or dace. It seems that the pike put the roach off all along the stretch. I want to catch roach so I've got to get rid of the pike; but I need to catch a roach in order to do so. These things *always* happen when I've got no spoons or plugs with me!

I nearly always manage to get a couple of gudgeon, however, and I find these are often better than traditional livebaits anyway. Most gravelly stretches hold gudgeon and you would think it a simple matter to pick up a few on float tackle with the bait bumping along the bottom. But how often it doesn't work out that way!

One way I have found which is an almost certain winner on the waters I fish is to leger for them. Leger for livebait? Believe me, I've caught more gudgeon on leger than on anything else. If they're able to pull my rod tip round when I'm legering for barbel I don't see why they can't when I want some livebaits. And, in fact, it's a very practical method of getting livebaits. Using a No. 14 hook and about three maggots you can't fail to hook them if the bites come. And there's no mistaking them when they do, either!

### Deadbaiting

There is one method of pike-fishing which really gives me an immense thrill and that is the now more commonly known deadbait method.

This is a method which has evolved during the post-war years and due to several articles which I wrote on the subject it has proved very popular and very deadly. I do not claim the discovery or invention of it, although I think I can rightly claim to be the first angler to develop it into a practical method, to experiment with it on many waters, both still and moving, and to publish the findings of those experiments in the angling press. Since the method has become more known it has accounted for many large pike.

Many years ago Edward Spence wrote in *The Pike Fisher* about some pike he caught by accident on deadbaits fished on the bottom but he obviously dismissed it as being 'one of those things' and not worthy of more than a few words' mention.

My brothers and I discovered in 1950 that pike would pick up a deadbait which was lying on the bottom of a small lake we often used to fish. At first we thought it was a fluke but later decided that it was due to the fact that livebaiting was carried out extensively on this particular lake. Our theory was that due to the inevitable large numbers of livebait casualties and the number of dead fish taken from overcrowded bait cans and thrown into the water, the pike would have got quite used to finding dead fish in the lake. Many of them of course would have floated, but an equal number would have sunk and what more natural place for a pike to find a dead fish than on the lake bottom? We decided that a dead fish on the bottom would look more natural than a half-dead livebait dangling from a bright red float on a piece of wire. We were right, and the number of pike we caught that way proved it. There were problems of course, and we didn't solve them all at once, but over a period of years we worked things out to our satisfaction, then tried the method out on waters where *no* livebaiting was done and it was just as successful!

At first I had difficulty in hooking the pike due to the way the bait was presented and after trying several ideas I settled for two trebles mounted on single-strand wire like an ordinary tandem tackle (*Figure 20*). One was placed in at the gills of the bait and the other about half-way along the body. The wire was then threaded through the remainder of the body and out at the tail. No weights at all were used

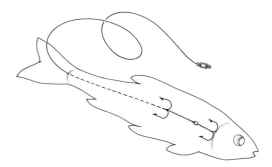

*Figure 20*   Method of fixing deadbait. Thread with baiting needle along dotted line

and it was found that in this way the bait *always* sank, with the hooks downwards and consequently out of sight. A small point, and maybe unnecessary, but I see no point in advertising the presence of the hooks when they can just as easily be concealed. With this hook tackle, used with a fixed-spool reel, it is as well to strike fairly quickly as it does not take a pike long to swallow a deadbait completely. If you are in any doubt you can use the same tackle, set farther back nearer the tail, leave the pick-up of your reel 'off' and strike when the pike has completed the first run.

Sometimes the bait will be picked up and taken with a tremendously long run and I do not know how to advise you to strike. Nearly always when this happens, the pike has the bait in its mouth and just appears to be trying to put as much distance between itself and its comrades, like a chicken jealously guarding a prize worm! If you wait too long, the distance between you and the pike will be too great to drive the hooks home effectively. I can only suggest that you strike *before* the distance becomes too great. I am firmly of the opinion that a big bait is the best bait for a big pike. I do *not* say that small baits *won't* catch a big pike, but what I *do* say is that big baits *can't* catch small pike. If however you are using a big bait and you find that it is picked up, dropped, picked up again, etc., but not fairly taken, the answer is a small pike and the solution is a smaller bait. If you haven't got a smaller one, don't worry, just cut the tail end off your big one and hook it on as before.

All the popular baits used by livebaiters may be used just as successfully dead, but if there is any shortage of baits (and there very often is a shortage on pike waters) herrings can be used with deadly effect. In fact I think they are more acceptable to the pike than the natural resident fish. They are different, they are easy to procure, they stay on well and pike like them! They can be bought in a variety of sizes – and I favour the Norwegian herring for size. You can get them up to about 1 pound weight and I find these ideal for pike over the 10 pound mark.

I said earlier that I preferred a large bait for large pike, but I would be hesitant to use a pound roach as a deadbait! It appears that you can kill and use as bait as many small roach as you like, without upsetting anyone, but the moment you suggest using say, a 2 pound chub, you are immediately in the dog-house. I wonder why. That 2 pound chub will almost certainly be the only bait you will use all day and you will be fairly sure that if it is taken you will catch a big pike.

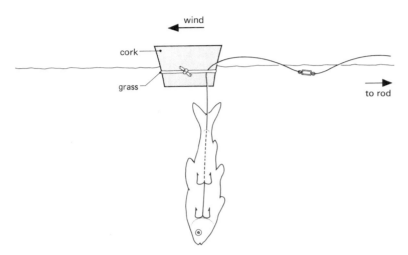

*Figure 21*　Method of sending out a large deadbait when the wind is favourable. When over a desired spot, a sharp strike breaks grass binding and releases bait

What I hope to try some time is a dead pike of about 5 pounds for a real monster!

The main difficulty with large baits is the difficulty in casting. I like to use a rod of the Mk 4 calibre when pike-fishing but though this rod is capable of mastering a large fish, it cannot be expected to cast a heavy bait. Even a herring is too large to cast properly and the strain put on the rod when casting one is terrific. You can overcome this difficulty by leaving the rod in the rest with the reel pick-up 'off' and using a sturdy stick to cast your bait. Cut a stout stick with a forked end, and lay the trace in the V meanwhile holding the line close to the stick. You will find that you can cast a very heavy bait in this manner and still be able to use a flexible rod with which to strike and play your pike.

Another way of getting a large bait out is to tie it to a large piece of cork by means of a piece of grass and allow the wind to take it out for you (*Figure 21*). The rod remains in the rest and line is paid out until the cork has reached the desired spot. A sharp strike will then break the grass, release the cork, and allow the bait to sink. On the whole though long casting is seldom necessary. Pike haunts are as a rule not too far out, and usually in the vicinity of rush or reeds. Sometimes pike like to frequent the deeper water out in the middle of the lake (usually under cold or windy conditions) and it is then that the long casting becomes necessary.

This method of pike-fishing is equally effective on lakes, rivers, pits, canals and reservoirs. Some may find it uninteresting to watch a line hanging from a rod tip into the water and wait for it to move, but to carp-fishers it will be nothing unusual. If you like to see a float go under, there is no reason why you should not use one and it doesn't *have* to be a large bung. Alternatively you can clip your rod into a bite alarm and carry on roach-fishing until the buzzer gives you warning that something's afoot.

Serious study of your waters will give you a better idea of where to find your pike than I can tell you, but it is possible to use 'groundbait' to attract your pike. Chopped-up herrings or sprats scattered in the vicinity of your deadbait will often bring a lot of pike into the swim – especially on mild drizzly days; pike seem to be on the move quite a

A big Wotton pike taken on a deadbait

lot under these conditions, but their movements are not heralded by swirls and strikes as they often are on brighter days. The deadbait method is not so effective on those bright 'summer's day in winter' type of days but it comes into its own again when the water is very cold. It is said that pike do not move under cold conditions, but I think this is wrong. I think they move *more slowly* under cold conditions. Consequently they may be reluctant to chase a spinner, but will glide slowly over to a dead fish and shovel it up off the bottom.

A lot has been written about the freshness of baits, and it has been advocated that the best spinnning bait for pike is a freshly killed fish. Having many times used baits which were positively stinking and found them just as successful as freshly killed baits, I say that there is no foundation in it. The only advantage a freshly killed bait has, that I can see, is that it will stay on the hooks better if it is being used as a spinning bait. If it is being used stationary, fished on the bottom it doesn't matter a scrap! If you are ever short of bait – take a stroll round the margins and you'll often find enough small dead fish floating there to last you all day. If someone tells you that a moving bait is necessary to catch pike, and that a dead fish catches no pike (it's been said plenty of times before), go to your fishmonger's, buy a couple of pounds of herrings and prove him wrong. It is a fascinating way of catching pike and I'm convinced that once you try it you'll do less livebaiting.

More recent experiments with deadbaits fished on the bottom have proved to be of great interest. Although still virtually a static method it was found that many more baits were taken if they were inched very slowly along the bottom. This only applies to waters with clear weed-free bottoms and then only on certain occasions. The reasons for this are not very clear but it is a method well worthy of consideration when all else fails. Generally speaking, however, the numbers of fish lost through not being properly hooked are rather high and more experiment is necessary.

Since this chapter was first written, great strides have been made in the use of artificial lures, deadbaiting techniques have improved, new rigs have been developed, pike-fishing has become more specialized, and it has been established that pike feed well at night even in the depths of winter. We are, perhaps, also beginning to fish for our pike in a style similar to that described as 'sport-fishing' by our American friends. We are learning how to fish deep waters with the use of transistorized

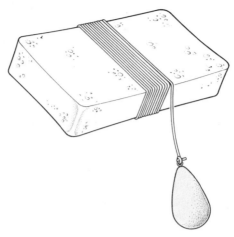

*Figure 22*    Marker buoy

sonar units. We are learning to chart the bottom and locate likely pike lies. We have devised or copied such ideas as the oblong block or 'flip-over' marker buoy. This is simply a block of foam or an empty can roughly the shape and size of a housebrick around which is wrapped 100 or so feet of cord. A heavy lead is attached to the cord, and when the whole is tossed overboard the weight turns over the block on the surface. When the weight has reached the bottom, the 'turn-over' stops and the spot is marked accurately. The marker cannot drift off course. This is an extremely good method of marking a pike hot spot. *Immediately* a fish is hooked from a drifting boat the marker rig should be tossed overboard. When the fish is finally beaten, the boat may have drifted 100 yards from it.

Short crank-handled bait-casting rods are being used more today than ever before. These, because their accompanying multiplying reels hold heavier lines than traditional fixed-spool reels, are possibly more suited to boat-fishing with plugs and other lures. Accurate short casts can be made with them but they can also be used for less accurate distance work.

Small spoons, offset spinners, and jigs, are better fished with a light fixed-spool outfit. They require a light line to achieve distance and a short wire trace or leader is essential. The last two named can be retrieved through remarkably snaggy water because their hooks ride with the point uppermost. The offset spinners should be used with a

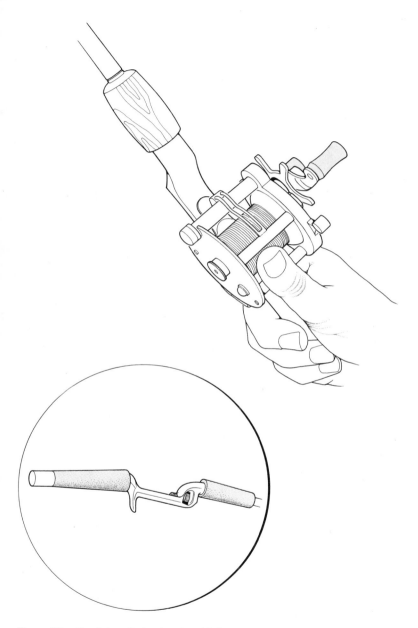

*Figure 23*  Crank-handled rod and multiplier reel

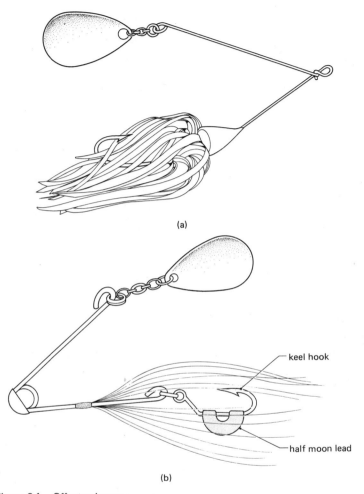

(a)

keel hook

half moon lead

(b)

*Figure 24*   Offset spinners
A Commercial offset spinner
B Home made offset spinner using large safety-pin

steady, unbroken retrieve. So handled, they will pass through a veritable jungle of roots or underwater branches without fouling. Breaking the retrieve causes the lure to 'collapse' and the chances of snagging are increased. Jigs do not work extremely well on wire leaders but their up-and-down action (as described in the perch chapter) is deadly for small pike.

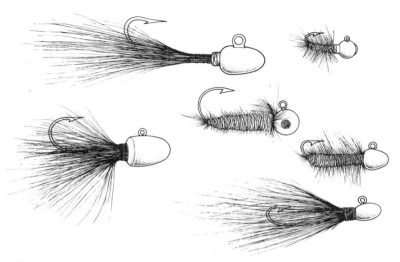

*Figure 25* American lead-head jigs in variety. These lures are deadly for perch and useful for pike

We are also beginning to understand plugs a little more. It is my opinion that life is too short to understand them all but I think we can divide them up into five different categories. There are those that work on the surface; those that dive a few feet when retrieved; those that dive deeply when retrieved; those that sink slowly; and those that sink quickly. Vanes, diving heads and propellers give them their actions and make them attractive for their own prescribed conditions.

The first three mentioned are, to me, the most popular, most effective, and certainly the easiest to understand; and yet for years I have been seeing them used incorrectly.

Surface plugs for example, are designed purely and simply to be worked on the top. The Americans call them 'top-water' plugs and they talk of 'top-water' fishing. In Britain they work best in calm-water situations. They are relatively ineffective in a chop or ripple, but when made to gurgle, splutter and pop on an unruffled surface, the effect they can have on pike is remarkable. To see a pike throw itself out of the water, hang on to a surface chugger and shake its head in anger before returning with an almighty splosh, is to enjoy action fishing at its best. To feel the light rod buck as the hook sets and the fish tail-walks and trampolines 20 yards out has to be experienced to be

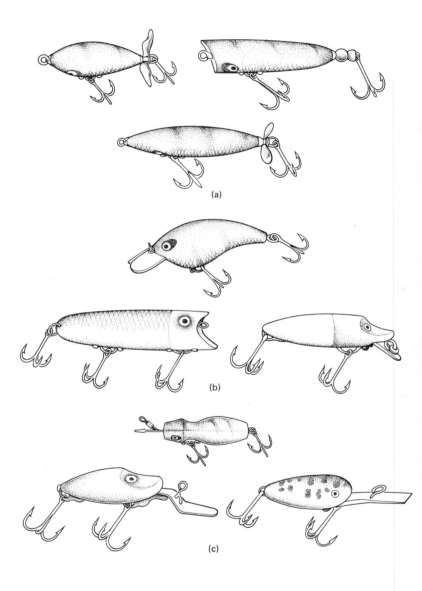

(a)

(b)

(c)

*Figure 26*   The three main plug types
        A   Surface lures
        B   Shallow divers
        C   Deep divers

believed. But it only happens if the surface lure is fished correctly. It has to be cast, twitched, left, twitched and left again so that it disturbs the surface with a series of noisy pops and gurgles. *It is as likely to be taken when completely still as when on the move.* Each cast has to be fished out unhurriedly; surface lures churning crazily in a straight line are seldom taken.

There are days when every pike in the lake appears to be on the move. Accumulations of small roach or rudd near the surface make them strike violently, picking up several fish en route, and possibly leaving others wounded on the surface. Timing the cast is difficult, but if you can drop a surface popper into those widening ripples and leave it there, giving it the occasional twitch, the pike may take it when it returns to mop up the remnants.

These tactics obviously work better in the early part of the season and are unlikely to succeed when waves lap the banks and the water is near to freezing. There are times, towards the end of the season, however, when mild weather and an early sun make the water come to life. I have occasionally used surface lures successfully in February and March, but I cannot recall having caught fish on them during January or December. I have never expected to do so.

It *is* important to remember that a surface lure is just that and nothing more. Putting a lead weight uptrace and using it as an underwater plug may work occasionally, but there are other lures more suited to the task. If it has a hollowed out head or propellers fore and/or aft, it is almost certainly a surface plug and should be used as such.

Shallow divers that float when at rest are recognizable either by a steeply angled diving vane or an angled groove at the head. These lures are really better if fished without a heavy wire trace. They are designed to be fished without swivels and ironmongery. Many Americans tie them directly to the reel line; others use a simple snap.

There is perhaps just cause in Britain for the use of a short snap-swivelled leader. It makes for an easier lure change and it reduces the risk of lost fish. American bass do not have teeth like our native pike, and although the action may be slightly impaired by the use of a wire leader it is better to be safe than sorry. Especially with expensive lures.

Again the lure should not be encumbered with lead of any kind. It will dive when the retrieve is started; it will rise up to the surface when the retrieve is stopped. The faster the retrieve the deeper the lure will dive – up to its maximum of around 3 feet. After that speed will make no difference and possibly render the lure less effective. Often it will be taken when the retrieve has been stopped and its natural buoyancy is taking it up to the surface again. These 'hits', however, because of slack line, often end up as 'misses'!

Shallow divers are extremely good lures for boat-fishing and for searching shallow bays and overhangs. They may snag frequently but never at any great depth and a complete slackening-off may cause them to come popping to the surface again.

One important point to remember when fishing a shallow diver is to speed up the retrieve in the event of a 'follow'. Pike often follow lures without taking them. It just so happens that when a shallow diver is being used, the 'follow' can be *seen*. How many 'follows' take place in the depths when other lures are employed we shall never know. If a shallow diver is stopped or slowed down in order to 'encourage' the pike to take, the chances are it will be refused. A following pike is a cautious pike, but it may be fooled into grabbing something that looks like escaping.

Many surface and shallow-diving lures come armed with what appears to be too many hooks but, in my experience, removing a treble from any part of the body or tail end tends to spoil the action considerably.

Deep divers, though possibly less dramatic in performance, are ideal for use in deep still waters and (though this fact may not have been considered) for use in fast, deep rivers. Retrieved at speed or against the current of a river like the Hampshire Avon, Stour or Test, they will dive to their maximum depth quickly and remain on that level until the cast has been completed. Only when almost back to the rod will they rise to the top under pressure. They will, of course, come surfacewards if the retrieve is stopped completely, though a tight line will often hold them down, vibrating in one spot in a river. This particular tactic has often been employed successfully in a known salmon lie.

Deep divers are recognized by their near-horizontal diving vane. Often it is large in area like a flattened spoon; almost invariably it continues along the same plane as the body of the lure. Newcomers to plug-fishing are often deceived by this particular characteristic. They assume (and it is a natural assumption) that steeply angled vanes are the ones that make for deep diving. Like those already mentioned, deep divers float at rest and, depending upon design, will dive to 12 or more feet when retrieved. They are expensive and they are not recommended for use in overgrown waters. Once a bottom snag has been contacted the chances of pulling free are minimal. Hard pulling seems only to embed the lure more firmly. They are excellent lures for clean-bottomed gravel pits, however, and a special technique, which can best be described as one of 'fits and starts', can be deadly even in the depths of winter. The water must be shallower than the maximum dive depth, and once the lure has reached bottom, quick turns of the reel handle will make it dive and dig causing little spurts of sand or mud to emerge in its vicinity.

Few pike anglers can have failed to see the little clouds of mud stirred up either by an attacking pike or an escaping bait fish, and I can say with all honesty that there are days when this ploy pays big dividends.

In deeper water the same technique can be applied to either slow sinkers or fast sinkers, but there is a limit to the depth at which it can be effective. I *have* caught pike at depths below 25 feet but only once on a lure. It was a chromium pirk being 'deep trolled' accurately at that depth. I believe that its brilliance was the main reason for its being taken and I am of the opinion that, for really deep lure-fishing, those divers with a brilliant metallic finish are the ones most likely to be taken.

Experiments regarding colour may well be of benefit to lure-fishers and, while I would not be prepared to make rash predictions, I believe there is much truth in what is often called the 'spectrum theory'. Briefly, and with possible exceptions, it means that colours at the blue end of the spectrum show up at depths much greater than those at the red end. Red is reputedly only visible to a depth of around 12 feet; blue shows up at depths in excess of 100 feet. This theory is of interest only as a guide and as a possible thought-promoter, however. Understanding the actions and functions of the various lures is of much greater importance.

We would appear to have made great strides since those first early days of the legered deadbait. Long-range rigs, quick-strike tackles, specialized rods, huge landing nets, very special unhooking gags and pliers and other worthy items of tackle have been developed. Many have been developed with thoughts of pike conservation in mind – which is how it should be. It remains a fact, however, that deadbait-legering as such has changed very little *as a method* since those early days. It is still the same basically simple method. The only improvement I have been able to bring about has been to prove

Small pike on light tackle can be fun

exclusively that it works well after dark. I have not practised it often, but I can remember very few failures in this particular field. Generally speaking the average size of pike caught has been greater than those caught during the day. After gut-hooking several because bite indication was poor, I changed over to single-hook rigs with more losses but fewer damaged pike.

Fly-fishing with big streamer and bucktail flies took my fancy for a while and I do not complain if I catch pike on flies when fishing for trout. I like pike to eat too, and those from the trout reservoirs are 'extras'.

Today I enjoy fishing for pike with ultra-light rods, fine lines and tiny lures. I catch mostly small pike and do not hope to catch many big ones, but since I have already caught some big ones it does not matter. I have fun catching fish on tackle that allows them to fight their weight.

# 17 Barbel

## Feeding habits

Normally one associates barbel with big rivers, fast runs, weir races and deep turbulent pools. They are undoubtedly lovers of fast water at certain times of the year but modern angling methods have taken them from slow and almost still, eddies and slacks.

They are mainly bottom-feeders and obtain a lot of their food by turning over stones or grubbing in the gravel of the clean-bottomed reaches. Sometimes they will tuck themselves away under the bank and rest silently in the steady current, intercepting food as it comes down to them in the stream. In weir pools and areas directly downstream of them they will suck away at the algae-covered stones and piles, collecting many small creatures in the process. Loose pieces of silkweed washing off the weir apron also form part of their diet.

Much of the barbel's food is located by the four feelers or barbules situated at each corner of the mouth. These barbules are sensitive and help in the search for food at night when barbel often feed enthusiastically.

In very hot weather they may be heard making sucking noises in the streamer weed which rises to the surface in many faster-moving rivers. At times the weed may be seen to lift clear of the water as a barbel rolls, apparently on to its back, and sucks with a loud 'kissing' sound, some small item of food from its midst. It is almost impossible to see exactly what movement the barbel makes but there seems to be little doubt that it is a feeding action. I have heard from time to time of barbel being taken by presenting a surface bait to them while they were behaving in this fashion. So far I have never been able to do it myself, but I am convinced that it is quite possible despite the barbel's underslung mouth which does not seem to suggest surface feeding. One does not consider the barbel to be a winter-feeding fish and so the tactics described in this chapter will apply mainly to summer and autumn fishing. Barbel will of course feed in winter, but one does not

Bill Watson displays a north-country barbel

normally set out to catch them exclusively at this time of year. Those that are caught are usually caught by accident. In times of heavy flooding they are often disturbed and forced to leave their winter quarters and having done so they feed from time to time but summer and autumn are the accepted times to seek them. (Anglers like Fred Towns, John Everard, Peter Drennan and Peter Stone of Oxford have established that barbel often feed at dead of night in winter. When all boat traffic ceases and towpaths become deserted, the barbel in many Thames swims appear to 'come on feed'. Some of the catches compiled by these anglers have been remarkable and double-figure fish have been recorded. Touch-legering techniques are used and the fishing is practised without lights.)

Many rivers in this country do not hold barbel. Others hold them in numbers so small that they are hardly worth pursuing. But they are present in the Avon, Stour, Kennet, Thames, Yorkshire Ouse, Nidd, Swale, and Wharfe. They have been introduced to the river Severn and have flourished there. Extremely large barbel exist in a number of rivers and in many cases a special approach is apparently necessary for their capture. I shall discuss these big barbel later in this chapter, though it is doubtful if I can advise on how to catch them.

### Tactics

I have not caught many barbel on float tackle and those that I have caught have been accidental, but large numbers of big barbel are caught each year from the Royalty fishery by anglers using very fine float tackle. Their baits have been maggots and their tactics have been to feed the swim continually, often for days at a time, with loose maggots. Hundreds of gallons of maggots are thrown into the Royalty fishery each week, and it is understandable that the fish there have become accustomed to accepting them as their normal diet. This has led to the belief in many circles that the best way to catch barbel is to use a fine tackle, small hooks and single maggot baits, combined with the process of continually feeding the swim with loose maggots. It is probably the best way to catch Royalty barbel, but it is not by any means the best way to catch barbel from all waters!

There can be no doubt that the introduction of large quantities of loose maggots will often start barbel feeding. I have seen a shoal of barbel lying quite still and obviously not interested in food, suddenly become stimulated into feeding when maggots have been introduced above them so that a continual stream has passed amongst them. Sometimes the barbel react quickly, other times it takes several hours of continual baiting before they respond.

Having stirred them into activity, it is logical, I suppose, to expect them now to be interested in maggots coming down to them singly, and that the most likely bait would be a single maggot on a very small hook. This is the line of thought the Royalty experts take and this is how they catch their barbel – by drifting a single maggot to them on a very fine float tackle. The only fault I have to find with the method is that invariably a lot of big barbel are hooked and lost. I don't believe in leaving hooks and lengths of nylon in any fish if I can help it! I want to land all the fish I hook, and while I know that this is impossible, I can, and do, at least, make sure that the tackle I use gives me a reasonable chance.

If the continual use of maggots causes fish to become preoccupied with them exclusively, it is reasonable and sensible to fish with single maggot hookbaits, but, in my experience, this is not necessary with barbel. I have caught scores of barbel in maggot-baited swims, but I have caught them on bunches of maggots, legered on No. 8 or 10 hooks, tied direct to lines of up to 7 or 8 pounds breaking strain. The line strength I use depends upon the location and the size of the fish expected, but I seldom use lines of less than 5 pounds breaking strain.

I found that simple leger tackle using the swan shot link will usually serve for practically all forms of barbel fishing. It will serve in fast weir pools and in the slower reaches of the Upper Thames where barbel are prolific but not sought after by many anglers. It will serve for far-off or close-in fishing and it will suit all baits.

Whenever the leger is used it is better, I find, to overcast and tighten up into the swim, or to cast well across the river and let the bait roll into it. It is not wise to cast directly to the desired spot.

Variations of all leger techniques may be employed in barbel-fishing and the number of baits which may be used successfully is quite astonishing. I have never been able to learn why one bait will be successful on a certain water and yet be practically useless on another. There are Thames backwaters and certain lengths of main river in the upper reaches which are often spoken of as being 'sausage waters'. That is to say, the only really successful bait used there is a piece of boiled sausage! On rare occasions the barbel there have accepted cheese and paste and, on the odd occasions, pieces of cooked meat, but most of the fish have been caught on sausage baits. Nowadays the dace, roach, bream, and chub in these stretches also take sausage baits. This is but one example of the success of a particular bait. At first one suspects that its success is entirely due to the fact that this bait is extensively used, and it is true that the anglers who leger there use little else. But there are hundreds of other anglers who use more orthodox baits such as maggots, worms and bread crust. It is strange that they seldom, if ever, come into contact with the barbel.

There are waters where the best bait is undoubtedly a big lobworm. There are others where the maggot reigns supreme. Many of these waters do not produce large numbers of fish and to contact one barbel in a day is to have done well. It is fairly safe to say that if the recognized 'best' bait does not produce a fish, it is unlikely that anything else will. Such is the way of these waters.

Smaller rivers like the Kennet, however, and in particular certain reaches of that river, hold larger numbers of barbel and it is most important, in my opinion to have a variety of baits. From the Kennet I have taken barbel on a score of different baits ranging from maggots to live minnows and from brandlings to breadcrust. Each time I have caught a barbel on a 'new' bait it is because I have not been able to catch them on any of the 'old' ones.

Barbel are strange creatures; hard to understand. One day the slightest shadow or footfall will scare them, another they will take not the slightest notice of half a dozen anglers walking the banks.

I have caught barbel at all hours of the day and night and I have probably caught more *after* nine a.m. than before. I have not found it necessary to rise early (unless it was to claim a special swim) for barbel, but I would certainly not advise against it.

If I had to choose a time to fish for barbel I would probably choose the last two hours before sunset and the first two hours after, but this would only apply during the summer months. In autumn I believe you are likely to catch barbel at any time of the day provided you know where they are.

I do not believe it is necessary to go into great detail regarding methods of barbel-fishing. In most waters the simple legering techniques (described on pages 48–53) will suffice. It will seldom be necessary to fish extremely fine and, generally speaking, barbel bites on leger are unmistakable. There will come times, however, when the barbel do not take the bait decisively but simply mouth it very gently. This action does not result in any registration on the rod tip but it *does* send a trembling sensation along the line. If you are holding the rod and the reel line is looped over the index finger (or held lightly between the thumb and forefinger of the left hand) you will feel it 'buzzing'.

The problem is knowing what to do. If you wait, there's a chance that the barbel may pick up the bait and pull the rod tip round, but you can never be sure! And waiting sometimes means a lost opportunity!

One good thing about it all, however, is the fact that, although these registrations are very slight, the barbel are not terribly difficult to hit. The registrations are brought about by the barbel's large, underslung mouth toying with the bait. A firm strike at this moment usually results in the hook being driven home into the leathery lips; and once home it seldom comes adrift.

As with many other species of fish, it is often advisable to try a change of bait and natural baits such as crayfish, mussels and minnows are all worthy of consideration as well as the more orthodox and generally accepted baits.

**Big barbel**

Many anglers today are attempting to make a special study of the habits of big barbel and it is thought by some that it is only a matter of time before the present record is broken. I wonder if we can truthfully say that we're making any real progress?

Speculation continues as to whether certain waters do or do not hold record specimens and there still seems to be doubt in the minds of some anglers as to whether the record-sized fish, reported by others as having been *seen*, really exist or whether they are gross exaggeration.

Once it used to be thought that the Royalty fishery offered the best chance of a record. Later, when the tales of the Throop monsters were discussed it was thought that perhaps here, too, was a water which could produce a record-breaker. There arrived a period when anglers who simply wanted to catch barbel fished on the Royalty fishery. But those who had their sights on a record transferred their attention to Throop.

I have never been in any doubt about there being record-breakers in Throop. The snags and problems involved are well known but there can be no doubt at all that the fish are there. Enormous barbel have been taken from there by salmon-anglers and one ought to be able to fish there with some sort of confidence. But things tend to get out of perspective!

The truth is, of course, that there aren't many really big barbel *anywhere* except, perhaps, the Royalty. Let's think in terms of fish over 10 pounds for a moment and forget record-breakers for the time being. The vast majority of barbel over 10 pounds are caught each year from the Royalty and everyone talks of the 'Avon barbel'. But where else along the Avon are 10 pounders caught?

There *are* barbel in many parts of the middle Avon and tremendous fish they are too, but they are widely scattered and very difficult to catch. Royalty tactics simply will not catch these fish although it is generally believed that they would. Ever since Mr Charles Cassey caught his 16 pounder from Ibsley on salmon tackle, there has been great speculation regarding record-breakers from the middle Avon. And speculation is about as far as we've got!

I've had some experience of the middle Avon and, while I'm not prepared to state whether there are bigger barbel there than in the Royalty, I am prepared to say that I'm sure a 20 pounder is possible. I have stood and trembled as I've watched a shoal of barbel containing fish of such dimensions that I could hardly believe this was happening to me! I have seen a shoal of fish, five of which would have beaten the existing record and the largest of which was *at least* 20 pounds. I've watched them for hours and I've gone back to see them next day and they've been gone. I've searched the river day after day to try and locate them and suddenly they've reappeared in the same place. Now, I've always regarded finding the fish as a battle half won. 'Find the fish first and then you can set about catching them,' has always been my war cry. Well it doesn't work in the middle Avon! At least it hasn't so far.

On most occasions the very act of fishing for them has made them disappear. Don't misunderstand me, they were *not* scared by waving rods or splashes of white shirts because I know better than to do this. I have inched baits into position with Dick Walker downstream lying on his belly giving directions. I've put those baits dead in the right spot to an inch. The barbel have swum over them and then leisurely disappeared! I could write a book about our schemes and dreams with those barbel. I could tell of massive baiting campaigns and countless hours of day- and night-fishing that resulted in two barbel – one 9 pounder and one about 9 inches! I could tell lots of stories but that is not the object of this chapter.

The object of it is to consider the problems of fishing for big barbel.

We can agree there are record barbel in the Avon and Stour. We know they are there because they can be seen. And I think we can possibly agree that big barbel you can see are not always extremely easy to catch!

Now, whether our middle Avon barbel were scared or not, it is significant that those we caught were both taken when we *couldn't* see them. That is to say dusk or later. I'm not going to press a case for night-fishing for barbel although I believe there *are* times and places where night-fishing offers the best chance. I am wondering, in fact, if waters where the barbel *can't* be seen might not be a better proposition.

Are there waters other than the Stour and Avon that could produce record barbel? I am in very little doubt that there are. The Thames and several of the Thames backwaters and feeders all contain enormous barbel. Fish of nearly 13 pounds have been taken, and huge fish have been hooked which substantial tackle has been incapable of holding. Several witnesses saw my brother lose a tremendous fish in the Thames in 1965. There's no doubt in their minds that this fish (it was in full view and only came adrift at the net) was a possible record-

Barbel from a Thames sidestream

breaker. How many such fish are there? What are the chances of catching one?

The first question must remain unanswered, for it is virtually impossible to locate fish by sight in the Thames. We cannot stand and wonder at shoals of barbel we can't see, but I believe there's enough evidence to show that big barbel are present in fairly large numbers in the Thames. And I believe that it's possible for the record to be broken from the Thames or its backwaters.

Discounting the Royalty fishery (which is a law unto itself) I would say that many more barbel come from the Thames than from the Avon. Not a few of them are in the 10 pounds plus class, and considering the number of anglers who fish for barbel on the Thames, the numbers caught are encouraging. Some barbel are also caught by accident, others are lost on tackle not suited to barbel-fishing, and I believe that if as many anglers fished the Thames in a style likely to catch barbel as there are fishing the Avon, the numbers caught would be astonishing. And one cannot help thinking about those fish which are lost.

A huge fish hooked and lost on the Stour or Avon could be a salmon. It could hardly be other than a barbel on the Thames (although the possibility of big trout must not be overlooked). So the answer to the second question must be that I believe there's as much chance of catching a record barbel from the Thames as there is from the Avon or Stour. And this despite the fact that I have been able to watch barbel on the Avon and Stour and not on the Thames. I do not, however, regard this as a disadvantage any longer. One has to fish 'blind' on the Thames and when I have discussed this in the past with keen Thames barbel-anglers we have tended to look upon this as important. We have thought that the Avon or Stour angler who can first locate his fish must be at an advantage. Today I do not think this is so. At least one can cheerfully fish on in a Thames swim never quite knowing whether the fish are there or not. One is not inclined to fish at all in an Avon swim which obviously does *not* contain fish!

Every season is different from the last, however, and there may come times when the Avon and Stour waters are coloured or in semi-flood during the accepted barbel fishing months. Then one's attitude must change.

And the thought of flood or semi-flood conditions reminds me that there must be yet another river capable of producing a record barbel. The river is, of course, the Kennet. Was not a barbel weighing 14 pounds 4½ ounces taken from the Kennet some years ago? The barbel came from deep slack. Once again the fish could not be seen, and I doubt if anyone realized that such big barbel existed in that particular stretch of water.

I have caught a lot of barbel from the Kennet and I have been attached to some very big fish which have broken me. I have also seen other anglers well and truly broken, and I believe that a record barbel could possibly come from the Kennet, even though I'm still not sure of the identity of the species which did the breaking. I can only say that those fish were more likely to be barbel than anything else.

And can we now afford to disregard the Great Ouse? It has never been considered a barbel river although good barbel have been caught there from time to time by accident.

Some years ago young anglers like Ian Howcroft and Chuck Nunn set out specifically to catch barbel from the Ouse. They succeeded on several occasions. The barbel they caught were comparatively small, weighing up to about 4 pounds but fish very much larger were hooked and lost. With more anglers fishing the Ouse using styles and tackles more suited to barbel-fishing it is conceivable that much bigger barbel will be caught from now on.

Like many other anglers I expect the barbel record to be broken, but I shall not be surprised if the fish comes from somewhere a long way from the Stour and Avon.

# 18 Perch

How many years is it since reports of big perch were regularly appearing in the angling press? How long is it since we were able to say with some authority and a degree of confidence that conditions were (or were not) right for *perch*-fishing? In fact, how long is it since we were able to set off on a fishing trip with thoughts *only* of perch in mind?

Those really *were* the days!

They ended in the 1970s when strange disease and mysterious deaths occurred in the perch populations of many waters. The transference of seemingly healthy fish from one water to another only served to cause the disease to spread more rapidly and hastened the end of the perch-fishing as I knew it in the 1950s and 1960s.

It was a sad blow and one which I felt very strongly because to me there was something rather special about perch-fishing.

But, with luck, the situation could soon be back to normal again. There are signs of perch revivals on many of my old waters and although many of the fish are still small, I believe they're going to make it. Perhaps some of the ideas I worked on with my brother Ken in those earlier years will still work today in waters where the perch have made a comeback.

Very few anglers ever set out to catch perch. There were a few dedicated specialists who took them seriously and who could, each season, produce proof of their specialization in the shape of top-quality perch. There are, no doubt, a few of those experts still around, but many of the big perch catches recorded have been accidental.

There was a time when I, too, developed such a liking for perch that I found myself sizing up new waters with regard to their perch-fishing potential, and after a while I found I could state with a fair degree of accuracy whether or not the perch were 'on' or 'off' on a particular day.

My best perch was an accidental $4\frac{1}{4}$ pounder but I have had several approaching 3 pounds and, I imagine, a hundred or so over 2 pounds, but while it's always enjoyable catching a big fish of any species, I have never seriously set out to catch *big* perch.

In the days when perch were plentiful I simply tried to avoid the hordes of little striped horrors that strangled themselves with unfailing regularity on baits too big for them to handle, and I used to think in terms of – say – $\frac{3}{4}$ pound and upwards. Those were the perch I tried to catch and I never yet found a way of being selective. A $\frac{3}{4}$ pound perch could manage almost anything a 3 pounder could manage – even if it choked itself in the process!

There was something exciting about early winter in those days because, with luck, the perch in several rivers and streams I fished would then be shoaled following the frosts and autumn rains. Several still waters I knew began to produce too. I fished for river perch of all sizes, and because it involved a fair amount of moving from swim to swim it was ideally suited to my temperament. I still enjoy it today – travelling light and searching.

My brother Ken and I developed a 'system'. We simply went from swim to swim trying a combination of worms and brandling baits fished on and off the bottom with float tackle. Sooner or later we would hit on the right spot, the right bait and the right presentation and start catching fish. We were fairly sure after the first fish that we would get more, and we were usually right. Find one small-river perch and you've likely found a shoal.

This isn't always true of perch earlier in the year, despite the fact that they are usually regarded as shoal fish. If you hit a school of tiny perch, of course, there's always a problem. You'll often just keep catching them the same size one after the other until you're sick of them. But if you locate a shoal of perch holed up in a small river in November, the chances are that you'll find variety. By fishing 'the system' it is possible to hook perch of all sizes, and the fact that the first few fish are veritable tiddlers is unimportant. The next fish could easily be a 3 pounder and the following one any weight in between.

It is not a difficult kind of fishing, and it demands little or nothing in the way of specialist tackle. In fact, I believe it is better to keep everything as simple as possible. Perch, if they bite at all, usually do so with a determination that leaves you in no doubt and there is no need whatsoever for sophisticated floats and shotting.

The float can be cocked by one shot somewhere near the hook and it isn't at all critical – *though the depth at which the bait fishes often is.*

Situations vary from water to water, of course, and no one can lay down anything concrete about where, how and when to catch perch, but, taking some of the better perch waters I have fished as examples, I think there are a few common factors worth considering.

Bulrushes and gravel are usually found together and they both indicate *possible* perch-holding spots. With thoughts in mind, therefore, that perch are likely to hole up in bulrush beds and that it is often necessary to tempt them out, the importance of simple tackle becomes immediately obvious.

The bait often has to be fished very close to the rush stems, and it is better to have as few shots as possible on the rig. One big shot comes clear of snags much easier than several small ones. A piece of peacock quill or a simple porcupine quill will serve as a float either for drifting down or laying on in a reasonable current. And it happens to be a fact that perch are seldom found in a current that isn't reasonable!

Hook size can range from 10 to 6. I doubt if it is necessary ever to go above or below these sizes in the normal course of events. If luck is with you and you find a biggish perch in the vicinity of a dense rush bed, you can usually be quite optimistic about the rest of the day. That is often the forerunner of a bag of reasonable-quality fish. But I'm very

Top quality perch caught by F.J.T., several over 2 pounds

undecided about what to advise in the event of it being an apparent 'loner'. My inclination is to move on after half an hour or so to try and locate another holding spot, but I have known occasions when it has paid to stay put and keep plugging away with the same bait . It has occasionally produced a brace of 2 pounders and made the long wait worthwhile.

The foregoing are simple perch-fishing observations, and the emphasis is indeed on simplicity. There *are* situations that call for special techniques but in my opinion they are few and far between. Location and recognition of conditions are more important, in my opinion, than technique.

When the perch of the Great Ouse were in their absolute prime during the early 1950s it was not uncommon for one or other of our little group to say, 'Today is a perch day! We can catch chub and roach some other time, but today is for perch.' And it was so.

It seemed that a mild November morning, beset by one of those fairly thick fogs that are sometimes referred to as dripping fogs (probably because they *do* drip and often turn to drizzle), was ideal.

Water level and colour played some part and it was better if the river was up a little and slightly coloured. High floods and thick water seldom produced perch in any quantity, although I know one small mill stream that still produces the occasional big perch (for the water) from floodwater slacks. But, although we were able to recognize good conditions when they came, we were never able to say in advance just what the perch wanted, or how they wanted it offered. We found that out by trial and error, by fishing at all depths with a moving lobworm, then a static lobworm and finally by anchoring the bait on the bottom. Then we repeated the whole procedure with brandlings or marsh worms. Somewhere along the line we usually found the right formula – if we tried enough spots. Strangely enough once we found the formula it seemed to work for the rest of the day – even in different swims. But it could quite easily change overnight. Perch that were taking – say – lobs laid on one day may easily have preferred brandlings fished at mid-water 'on the trot' the next day. There was no telling; but that's what made it fun. Whoever made first contact reported to the others – and it usually worked in all swims.

There were days, however, when perch in certain known swims simply refused to move out of cover and co-operate. Then we changed tactics briefly. For situations such as this we carried some small vibrating bar-spoons with violent actions that could be felt right through to the rod tip. Retrieved against the steady current, and running as close to the rush stems as sensible casting allowed, these spoons often had a remarkable effect on the reluctant perch. Occasionally one would dart out of cover and take the spoon without any preliminaries, but generally speaking our object was *not* to catch them that way. We found that the spoon's action was often quite sufficient to draw the perch out. We'd spot a striped back as the spoon was followed and that was enough. We knew then that there were perch close by and that we had started them moving. From then on we concentrated on worm-fishing but when the action slowed down we changed back to spoons once more. It was not unusual in those days to keep the fish coming one way or the other for hours at a stretch, and even though on most occasions they were a mediocre mixture, we always enjoyed catching those perch.

Once the perch shoals had formed (usually soon after the annual leaf fall) they remained fairly well bunched until a raging flood split them up. From then on location became more difficult, but given time it was sometimes possible to encourage accumulations in certain areas by baiting with chopped worms or brandlings. I recall baiting two swims one Friday evening with a large quantity of neat brandlings and catching my first perch from one of them on Sunday afternoon. But those two swims yielded about 30 pounds of perch during the next few hours.

I am encouraged to think that these times are about to return because of several recent observations on the same water, and I hope that my hopes will be realized. Recently, a couple of young anglers, fishing from the opposite bank in what used to be a recognized perch hole, caught fourteen perch ranging from about 6 to 14 ounces. Nothing very wonderful in their eyes, but I see it as an excellent sign for the future.

Friends of mine who fish the Upper Thames and who have not seen a perch there for a number of years are now reporting the occasional half pounder from spots where pounders were once common.

The Avon and some of its tributaries are producing perch once again — some of them already in the 2 pound category. It is possible, of course, that they never really disappeared from the Avon completely, but they undoubtedly went from the swims I used to exploit. Perhaps isolated pockets of them have always been present. If that is so, the time will come eventually when conditions are perfect for an extra-special perch spawning! The following year we'll

F.J.T. unhooks a big Avon perch

probably be driven crazy by hordes of tiny perch bent on suicide, but I promise I'll never complain about them again. Instead, I'll look forward to seeing them develop into bristling, aggressive pounders.

There are indications, too, that the perch have returned to several of the still waters I fish. They will present a few' more problems, of course, but it is good to think they are fighting back. They are sadly misunderstood fish. None of us really knows much about still-water perch but they are very interesting fish. I remember, of course, those days in the 1950s when, by legering deep at very long range, the massive perch of Arlesey lake were taken regularly by those who knew how to catch them, anglers like Dick Walker, Bob Rutland, Alan Brown and others. Those were big fish caught by intent and by methods designed to deal with a special situation. I came in at the tail end and missed all but the odd fish weighing a pound or so.

Like their river counterparts, still-water perch have seldom been sought intentionally and yet very reasonable average-sized specimens *could* be taken and *were* taken by the few who tried. I suppose few anglers bothered because of the large numbers of small, suicidal perch that were present in so many still waters.

The traditional places for perch were supposed to be near lock gates, camp sheathing, wooden piles and so on. It is true that perch could be found there, but mostly they were small and the chances of catching one above average were slender. But odd big fish *were* present, and still are in many lakes, pits and reservoirs.

They were not wiped out, and it is pleasing nowadays to stand on a jetty and see the shadowy shape of one big perch appear briefly in among the small ones hanging around the area. I have seen it several times and I am encouraged.

The odds against catching the big one today are probably a lot less than they were twenty years ago, but it was necessary then (and I believe it still is today) to fish for perch without too much thought about size. It is difficult to try and select a big perch from a shoal of tiddlers, but the shortage of perch today makes the task perhaps a little easier.

In the waters where I know perch have returned, there are fewer, but slightly better-quality fish. And, more importantly I think, there are still big old 'lone rangers' to be found around here and there.

I've felt this way for some time, and years ago it was not too unusual for brother Ken and me to fish for perch intentionally on one or two of the trout reservoirs.

Hanningfield had a bonanza perch crop for several years and while I didn't get the opportunity to fish there often, I did truthfully fish in a way which would in no wise deter the perch from taking. I won't say I fished with thoughts of *avoiding* trout, but I certainly did not try to avoid the perch either. I used hair, bucktail and feathered streamers, fished them deep, and picked up a few ideas about what patterns perch prefer.

At Pitsford reservoir, when perch were the subject for a certain amount of grumbling by the trout anglers, we once took out a boat and caught perch by intent. In fact, we asked around where most perch were being caught, headed for that area and had it all to ourselves. That was near the end of the season; the following year the perch were gone from both waters. The trout anglers were no doubt pleased and they can't be blamed for that, but I think it's a great pity that one fish should be regarded as so much superior to another. Perch do not fight as hard or as long as trout it is true, and they may not have the same eating qualities, but that is a matter of opinion. If I had the choice now between half a dozen 2 pound perch and the same number of trout, I'd take the perch. *Not* because I rate them higher, but because I've caught plenty of trout and can hope to catch more because of our well-developed trout fisheries. Perch have fine eating qualities too, and I hope the day is near when I can again take away a brace for the table without any feeling of guilt.

There are signs that this could be so, and I have pounced eagerly on every little piece of evidence that points to it.

Back in the 1950s I used to fish for perch in Wotton lakes by three methods. One could be loosely described as sink-and-draw fishing with worms, another was with small moving deadbaits, and the third was legering with small dead perch.

The third method was of little consequence, except that on the rare occasions when it worked, the fish were usually in the 2 pound plus bracket; but small pike were invariably troublesome.

The second method also attracted pike, but there were certain areas of shallow, rush-fringed water where perch accumulated and where I twice saw my brother Ken hook (and lose) the biggest perch I have ever seen. Both times it came off, I believe, because despite the perch's great size, the bait (a 5 inch rudd) was too big for really effective striking. I *know* a 5 inch fish is by no means too big for a monster perch (and I reckon this one weighed 7 pounds) to *take and eat*, but it is possible that the hooks were shielded on both occasions. All of which has made me think more and more about the fly-fishing possibilities.

Assuming that a 5 inch deadbait *is* too big, it is logical to use one a lot smaller, but this presents casting problems. You *can* stick some lead on, of course, but the bait never fishes quite the same if you do.

With a fly rod, however, and an appropriate streamer fly, dressed, if you like, to imitate a small perch, there's no real problem, particularly if you're boat-fishing.

Perch, where they exist, take flies regularly on trout waters, so there is no reason to believe that fly-fishing won't work on coarse-fish waters. I'm not trying to convert anyone to fly-fishing (and in any event it is no great problem to fish a streamer fly on a light spinning rod if you pinch a swan shot above it and use a fine line), but I do look upon it as a very useful means of catching perch. And perch hooked on fly usually stay hooked.

It will probably never work quite as well as the first-mentioned method, however, which involves casting very lightly leaded worms into deep, clear water over a gravel bar and retrieving them sink-and-draw style. Find a shoal of perch in such a situation on a mild winter's day and you can literally clean it out that way. At least you can if you don't lose a fish. That sometimes puts an end to it immediately!

I am very pleased to note that the perch are beginning to show again at Wotton lakes, and already simple float-fishing with worms is taking its toll. The best I've seen so far since their return is a mere 12 ounces, but time and the hordes of tiny rudd will surely tell!

At the end of the 1978 trout season, Little Tring reservoir produced a few perch around the pound mark, and the very last brown trout caught from there had a 3 inch perch inside it! There had obviously been a recent spawning and whether or not these perch will be welcomed by the trout-fishers really doesn't matter. It will be simple enough to transfer them to near-by Wilstone, Startops or Marsworth if necessary.

Meanwhile I see signs of the perch revival in local pits, ponds and shallow lakes. I've heard of the odd fish here and there from the local canal and, with any luck at all, 2 pounders will become fairly common again.

Jig-fishing, as practised in the USA for fish such as bluegills, bass and crappie, has proved highly successful for perch of all sizes. These jigs and weighted flies (tied to look like small fish in some instances and bearing no resemblance to any creature living or dead in others) can be cast and retrieved with a series of jerks to make them rise and fall attractively in the water. I have fished jigs extensively since 1966 and I have caught almost every fish that swims on them. Discounting gudgeon, the only two species I have failed to catch are carp (and I have been close!) and barbel. I would not *recommend* them for fish other than trout, sea trout, chub, pike and perch. It is with perch that, even in recent years, I have had the most success. I have teased and tempted fish over 1½ pounds from a wooden jetty in Lincolnshire. I have caught small canal perch, modest gravel-pit perch and several good reservoir perch both by jigging under the rod tip and by casting and retrieving.

To prove a point to an astonished John Mason at Wotton in 1978 I caught thirty perch in as many minutes by jigging underneath our anchored boat. The first fish took a pink-headed, white-haired monstrosity often referred to as the 'pink-headed shaving brush' (or the PSB) because it resembles just that. I changed to a different pattern at once and caught perch on ten different jigs. None was over 6 ounces, and all were as alike as peas in a pod. Obviously there had been a good spawning and later in the season fish in the 1 pound plus class were taken regularly.

Jigging is an extremely good 'search-and-find' method of perch-fishing. It *can* be practised in rivers but it is not always easy to jig and remain concealed. Where it really shines is when used from a drifting boat. Left to trail deeply behind and jigged up and down continually, the tiny lure is obviously deadly to perch. If practised with a silent electric motor in motion it can be used moving upwind as well as down. It is advisable to mark well the spot where the first fish is taken and if possible to anchor or hold the boat in that area. I have said little about this method of fishing because it is something that has to be tried and proved. I cannot explain the technique, nor can I explain the reason for its deadliness. I suggest, however, that you try it for yourself and then tell me just how incredibly effective it is.

# Index